MCP AI

A Developer's Guide to Building Next-Gen AI Agents with the Model Context Protocol

Written By
Charles Sprinter

Table of Contents

Part I – Introduction and Foundations

Chapter 1: The Model Context Protocol and the Rise of Agentic AI

1.1 The Evolution of AI Agents and the Need for Context

The rise of AI agents marks a fundamental shift in how we think about building intelligent systems. Early artificial intelligence applications—like rule-based chatbots or recommendation engines—were often designed with narrow logic and no true understanding of the broader context in which they operated. These systems lacked memory, adaptability, and the ability to reason across multiple interactions. But with the emergence of large language models (LLMs) capable of understanding natural language, generating structured outputs, and calling functions, the potential to create adaptive, autonomous agents has grown dramatically. However, as these agents began to proliferate, it became evident that without a shared context, they struggled to make coherent decisions across sessions, tools, and interactions. This is where the need for **structured context management**—and ultimately a protocol like MCP—comes into play.

In the traditional design of AI systems, context is often hardcoded or loosely passed between components, leading to brittle pipelines. Imagine a travel assistant AI that helps users book flights, hotels, and restaurant reservations. Without centralized context, each task—booking a hotel or looking up flights—becomes isolated. The agent might forget the destination it retrieved earlier, fail to apply user preferences consistently, or miss dependencies like check-in times. As more capabilities are added, the spaghetti of integration points grows. What starts as a manageable system quickly devolves into an unscalable mess. What's needed is a **standardized way** to preserve and exchange structured context across tools and services—an approach that treats context as a first-class citizen.

Let's walk through a hands-on illustration to ground this in a real-world pattern. Suppose you're building a weather-aware travel agent using an LLM. In a raw prompt-based implementation, you might do something like this:

```
# Prompt sent to the LLM
```

```
prompt = """User is flying to Paris next weekend. What's the weather
forecast, and can you suggest suitable clothes to pack?"""
```

This prompt works for simple cases but breaks when modularity is introduced. If a weather function or external tool is called, there's no structured way to pass the location, date, or user preferences unless they're manually extracted and re-prompted.

Now, contrast this with an agent using structured context and an MCP-style setup. First, the agent initializes a session with persistent memory, then calls a tool:

```
{
  "jsonrpc": "2.0",
  "method": "weather.getForecast",
  "params": {
    "location": "Paris",
    "date": "2025-06-15"
  },
  "id": "tool-req-01"
}
```

The returned result is stored in the agent's internal context store, which can then be referenced in downstream logic or prompts:

```
{
  "temperature": "22° C",
  "condition": "Partly cloudy",
  "advice": "Pack a light jacket and comfortable walking shoes."
}
```

The LLM doesn't need to reprocess the entire prompt chain every time. It simply accesses the structured result and integrates it into its next action. This pattern—where context is fetched, stored, and reused—is what enables scalability. Tools and prompts become composable. Developers no longer have to hardcode logic for every permutation of user requests. And most importantly, agents can reason over a growing, consistent pool of data.

In summary, the evolution of AI agents has highlighted a critical missing piece: structured, persistent, and shareable context. Without it, agents remain stateless and short-sighted. The Model Context Protocol answers this need by offering a developer-friendly, language-model-compatible framework to define, retrieve, and act upon context. As agents become more autonomous and integrated into production workflows, this kind of context architecture will no longer be optional—it will be foundational.

1.2 Why MCP? The Need for a Protocol Standard

As AI agents grow more capable—navigating APIs, invoking tools, retrieving documents, and reasoning across tasks—the need for a **unified, structured communication protocol** becomes non-negotiable. Without one, developers are left to stitch together ad hoc glue code, define their own JSON schemas, and guess how to persist agent context between operations. This approach doesn't scale. It increases fragmentation, introduces inconsistencies, and creates brittle systems. What's needed is a **standard protocol**—a language-agnostic, structured way for agents and tools to exchange information consistently. This is where the Model Context Protocol (MCP) comes in.

MCP isn't just another JSON schema or REST wrapper. It introduces an explicit contract between the agent (typically powered by a language model) and external systems it interacts with. This contract defines how to register capabilities, how to initiate sessions, how to invoke tools, and—most critically—how to track and reuse **context** across interactions. Without a protocol like MCP, agents lack memory across tool calls and can't reason reliably from one action to the next. With MCP, tools become discoverable, results are type-safe, and context becomes a shared, addressable object across the agent's decision-making process.

To make this concrete, consider a language model integrated directly with a raw HTTP API for fetching stock prices. Without MCP, you might prompt the model like this:

```
prompt = "Fetch the stock price of TSLA and tell me if it's a
good time to buy."
```

Then, your application parses the model output, detects the stock symbol, sends a request to an external API, and feeds the result back into another LLM prompt. This is a fragile loop: you rely on heuristic parsing, duplicate context, and have no clear interface between agent and system.

11

Now, let's do it the MCP way. First, define the external function as a tool in the MCP server:

```json
{
  "jsonrpc": "2.0",
  "method": "tool.register",
  "params": {
    "name": "getStockPrice",
    "description": "Returns the current price for a given
stock symbol",
    "parameters": {
      "type": "object",
      "properties": {
        "symbol": { "type": "string" }
      },
      "required": ["symbol"]
    }
  },
  "id": "register-tool-1"
}
```

Once registered, the agent can discover and invoke this tool in a structured, predictable way:

```json
{
  "jsonrpc": "2.0",
  "method": "getStockPrice",
  "params": { "symbol": "TSLA" },
  "id": "call-stock-1"
}
```

The MCP runtime tracks this invocation, captures the response in a structured form, and updates the agent's context store. This makes it trivial for the agent to refer back to the result later—e.g., to compare prices, look at trends, or take further action—without duplicating logic or rewriting prompts.

MCP standardizes **how** the agent asks for information, **what** it receives, and **where** that data lives within the agent's memory. This separation of concerns enables modularity, improves security through constrained input/output schemas, and makes logging, debugging, and observability much easier to implement.

In short, MCP provides a developer-first protocol that brings predictability and interoperability to AI agent architectures. Without it, every agent system becomes a custom tangle of bespoke code. With it, you gain a foundation for reusable, testable, and scalable components—built on a protocol that speaks the same language as your LLM.

1.3 MCP's Vision: Scalable, Interoperable, Context-Aware Agents

The Model Context Protocol (MCP) was not designed as a temporary patch or a niche tool—it was envisioned as the **foundational protocol** for building scalable, interoperable, and context-aware AI systems. As the capabilities of language models evolve, the systems around them must mature too. Developers are no longer wiring up toy apps or demo chatbots. They are orchestrating multi-step reasoning, fetching live data from APIs, invoking external tools, chaining tasks across multiple services, and persisting memory between sessions. This complexity demands structure, and MCP answers with a formal model that brings discipline to the agent ecosystem.

At the core of MCP's vision is **context-awareness as a first-class citizen**. Agents should not merely process inputs and generate outputs—they should understand what they've done, what tools are available, what information has already been retrieved, and what goals remain. MCP achieves this by explicitly tracking context across invocations and structuring tool interactions using formal specifications. It allows tools, resources, and memory to be surfaced through a consistent interface, which makes agent behavior traceable, explainable, and debuggable.

To see MCP's vision in practice, imagine building an AI assistant that helps users plan business trips. The assistant needs to check flight options, book hotels, retrieve travel policies, and generate a summary itinerary—all through structured, auditable steps. With MCP, each function—such as getFlightOptions, bookHotel, and getCompanyTravelPolicy—is registered as a tool using JSON-RPC:

```
{
  "jsonrpc": "2.0",
  "method": "tool.register",
  "params": {
    "name": "bookHotel",
```

```
    "description": "Books a hotel given location, date range,
and preferences.",
    "parameters": {
      "type": "object",
      "properties": {
        "location": { "type": "string" },
        "checkIn": { "type": "string", "format": "date" },
        "checkOut": { "type": "string", "format": "date" }
      },
      "required": ["location", "checkIn", "checkOut"]
    }
  },
  "id": "register-hotel"
}
```

Once registered, this tool is invoked in a structured call, and MCP logs both
the request and response:

```
{
  "jsonrpc": "2.0",
  "method": "bookHotel",
  "params": {
    "location": "New York",
    "checkIn": "2025-07-10",
    "checkOut": "2025-07-14"
  },
  "id": "book-hotel-1"
}
```

The response might include confirmation details, cost, and cancellation
policy—all of which are added to the agent's context store. This enables
follow-up queries like "Can I cancel my reservation for free?" without
needing to re-fetch or re-parse previous outputs. More importantly, MCP
ensures that every interaction is **typed, logged, and reversible**. This is a
massive step forward for developers building agentic systems where
reproducibility, security, and reliability are key.

MCP's vision doesn't stop at simple tool invocation. It enables composability
across vendors and services, turning the agent into a runtime that orchestrates
and reasons over context-rich workflows. As agents scale into enterprises
and cloud-native platforms, MCP provides the protocol backbone needed to
make them reliable, interoperable, and easy to govern. It's the difference

between scripting a chatbot and engineering a context-aware autonomous system.

1.4 Practical Use Cases Across Industries

AI agents are rapidly reshaping workflows across industries, but without a shared protocol like MCP, their capabilities remain fragmented and brittle. The Model Context Protocol unlocks consistent, reliable agent behavior by standardizing how tools, resources, and context are shared across systems. In this section, we explore how MCP-powered agents solve real problems in various domains—not in abstract, but with practical, concrete workflows that developers can relate to and extend.

In **healthcare**, for instance, an AI agent might act as a clinical assistant that reviews patient notes, queries a database of treatment protocols, and drafts a summary recommendation. With MCP, each of these steps— `fetchPatientHistory`, `queryTreatmentOptions`, and `generateClinicalSummary`—can be defined as structured tools. The agent maintains contextual memory so that details from the patient's file persist across tool invocations, enabling continuity in reasoning and reducing hallucination risks. Because MCP enforces parameter schemas and logs every call, it also ensures compliance and auditability—critical in regulated environments.

In **financial services**, MCP enables smart compliance assistants. Imagine an LLM agent tasked with reviewing trading activity, pulling related policy documents, and flagging anomalies. Tools like `getTradeData`, `fetchComplianceRules`, and `submitAlert` can be exposed via an MCP-compliant server. Developers no longer need to hardcode brittle logic; they simply expose structured tools with clearly defined parameters, and the agent can decide when and how to use them based on context. This architecture supports secure delegation of decisions, with the added benefit of transparency through MCP's built-in logging.

Even in **software engineering**, MCP is enabling next-generation developer copilots. A code assistant might use MCP to retrieve coding standards, analyze file diffs, generate pull request messages, or look up internal documentation. With each tool invocation clearly defined and traceable, engineering teams can extend the system safely, knowing that new tools or resources won't break existing flows. The protocol's JSON-RPC interface is language-agnostic, so whether your tools are built in Python, Go, or Rust, they can plug into the MCP server with minimal overhead.

These use cases all benefit from MCP's foundational strength: a standard for context propagation, tool invocation, and interaction logging. Whether you're deploying agents in logistics, retail, education, or enterprise SaaS, MCP enables predictable, testable, and scalable workflows that go beyond prompt engineering. It gives developers the foundation they need to build robust, context-aware agents in the real world—agents that don't just answer questions, but coordinate actions, enforce logic, and integrate deeply into organizational infrastructure.

1.5 How This Book Is Organized (Concept → Code → Deployment)

This book is structured to guide you through the journey of understanding, implementing, and deploying MCP-powered AI agents—from foundational theory to hands-on coding and finally to real-world production deployment. The progression has been deliberately designed to mirror how developers learn and apply new architectural paradigms: first by grasping the "why," then by mastering the "how," and ultimately by shipping solutions that scale.

We begin with the **conceptual foundations** of the Model Context Protocol (MCP)—why it was created, the problems it solves, and how it compares to other integration strategies in the AI ecosystem. These early chapters define the architecture, core components like tools and resources, and the protocol's design principles. If you're new to MCP or protocol-based AI agent design, this section ensures you get the full picture before touching any code.

The second part dives into **hands-on implementation**. You'll build both MCP servers and clients, exposing your own tools, data resources, and prompt templates. Every chapter here contains step-by-step instructions, complete and correct code examples, test cases, and practical walkthroughs. You'll learn how to integrate MCP with LangChain pipelines, autonomous agents like AutoGPT, and how to manage their behavior with observability tools like AgentOps.

Finally, we shift into **deployment and real-world applications**. You'll learn how to deploy your MCP systems on AWS, Azure, and GCP, taking advantage of native services for AI, scaling, and cost monitoring. You'll also explore architectural best practices, advanced context management techniques, and strategies for chaining and orchestrating multi-agent systems.

Each chapter ends with a short summary to reinforce key lessons and—where appropriate—includes a practical exercise to apply what you've learned. Whether you're a backend engineer building MCP servers, an AI engineer embedding context into your agent workflows, or a technical architect deploying scalable, policy-compliant AI infrastructure, this book will give you the knowledge and tools to deliver production-grade agent systems.

Chapter 2: MCP Core Architecture and Communication Patterns

2.1 MCP Hosts, Clients, and Servers

In the Model Context Protocol (MCP) ecosystem, understanding the roles of **hosts**, **clients**, and **servers** is essential to architecting and deploying interoperable AI systems. These components form the backbone of every MCP-powered interaction, enabling distributed agents to exchange structured context, execute tools, and retrieve resources in a standardized way.

At its core, an **MCP Host** acts as the orchestrator or gateway—typically embedded in an AI application or agent framework (like a chatbot or autonomous agent loop). The host is responsible for initiating protocol-compliant interactions: it issues method calls to registered MCP servers, receives structured responses, and integrates them into the agent's context or decision-making loop. In simple terms, the host is where the agent "lives" and thinks.

An **MCP Client** is the piece of software (often bundled within the host) that knows how to communicate using the MCP spec—specifically JSON-RPC 2.0. It's responsible for encoding requests (e.g., `tool.invoke`, `resource.get`) and routing them over HTTP or WebSocket to the correct server. Think of the client as the outbound communicator, wrapping and dispatching agent requests in a protocol-safe format.

An **MCP Server**, on the other hand, is where logic resides. Servers expose tools (functions that can be called), resources (data that can be fetched), and prompts (reusable language templates) through standard endpoints. A single server might offer a weather API wrapper as a tool, a financial dataset as a resource, or an enterprise support summary as a prompt template. Crucially, MCP servers advertise their capabilities through a `.well-known/mcp-discovery` endpoint, allowing hosts to discover what each server can do.

Let's walk through a basic flow. Suppose you have a LangChain agent running as the host. The agent's logic triggers a request to fetch the current weather based on the user's location. The MCP client in the host constructs a `tool.invoke` JSON-RPC payload and sends it to the MCP server. The server receives this call, runs the associated logic (e.g., calls OpenWeather API), and returns the structured result. The host integrates this result into the agent's prompt and continues the conversation—without ever needing to hard-code the data source or logic directly.

By clearly separating concerns—agent logic in the host, communication in the client, and logic/data in the server—MCP ensures clean architecture, modular development, and effortless plug-and-play behavior across distributed AI systems.

In practice, when building MCP systems, always start by defining your host's responsibilities, install or configure a client library, and register your backend logic as tools/resources in an MCP server implementation. This division is what enables real-world AI agents to scale, remain interoperable, and adapt rapidly to new data and services.

2.2 JSON-RPC-Based Workflows: Handshake to Invocation

In the Model Context Protocol (MCP), every meaningful interaction—from discovering what tools a server offers to invoking a specific function—is powered by JSON-RPC 2.0. This protocol underpins all communication between hosts (AI agents) and servers (providers of tools, resources, and prompts), offering a clean, predictable structure for request-response messaging over HTTP or WebSocket. To implement MCP correctly, developers need a firm grasp of the complete lifecycle of these JSON-RPC workflows: from the initial handshake, through capability discovery, to invocation.

The interaction begins with **discovery**, often initiated when the host loads or restarts. The host, via its MCP client, sends a `GET` request to the server's `.well-known/mcp-discovery` endpoint. This request is not a JSON-RPC call, but it returns a list of all supported methods, their schemas, and metadata. For example, a discovery response might reveal that a server supports a `tool.invoke` method called `"get_forecast"` which requires a `"location"` parameter. This discovery phase helps hosts dynamically understand what services are available, enabling plug-and-play extensibility without needing to hard-code server capabilities.

Once a tool is discovered, the client initiates a proper JSON-RPC **handshake**, starting with a `context.initialize` method. This registers the host session with the server and shares relevant metadata such as supported features or preferred communication modes. Here's a typical payload:

```
{
  "jsonrpc": "2.0",
  "method": "context.initialize",
  "params": {
    "session_id": "abc-123",
    "capabilities": {
      "streaming": true,
      "version": "1.0"
    }
  },
  "id": 1
}
```

If the server responds with a valid `result`, the session is ready for real interaction.

Next comes the **invocation phase**, where actual work happens. Suppose the host wants to retrieve a forecast. It sends a `tool.invoke` request with parameters discovered earlier:

```
{
  "jsonrpc": "2.0",
  "method": "tool.invoke",
  "params": {
    "tool": "get_forecast",
    "input": {
      "location": "New York"
    }
  },
  "id": 2
}
```

The server processes the call—perhaps calling a real-world API behind the scenes—and returns a structured response:

```
{
  "jsonrpc": "2.0",
  "result": {
    "output": "Rain expected in New York tomorrow."
  },
  "id": 2
}
```

Throughout the session, the host may continue to send `resource.get`, `prompt.fill`, or additional `tool.invoke` calls. Each request is structured the same way: using `method`, `params`, and a unique `id`. This consistency makes debugging, scaling, and automating MCP interactions remarkably straightforward.

In real implementations, JSON-RPC workflows allow MCP systems to remain stateless at the transport level but rich in contextual integration. Because each call is self-contained, agents can communicate with multiple MCP servers concurrently, retry failed calls with minimal overhead, and stream results when supported.

By adopting this strict, JSON-RPC-driven approach, MCP provides a future-proof, language-agnostic foundation that simplifies integration between LLM agents and real-world functionality—allowing developers to focus more on logic and less on orchestration complexity.

2.3 Security, Isolation, and Trust Boundaries

Security, isolation, and trust boundaries are foundational to the Model Context Protocol (MCP), especially when connecting large language model (LLM) agents to powerful external tools and data. Since MCP servers expose capabilities that can affect systems, retrieve sensitive data, or initiate side effects, they must be treated as privileged execution environments. Likewise, hosts (the LLM agents or applications invoking those tools) must be constrained, monitored, and authenticated to prevent misuse, abuse, or accidental invocation.

At a minimum, every MCP deployment must establish **clear trust boundaries** between three entities: the MCP host (e.g., an LLM client like Claude or OpenAI), the MCP client interface that negotiates with servers, and the MCP servers themselves. The client and server should never implicitly trust each other. Instead, they must authenticate each other and define capabilities in an explicitly scoped manner.

The first layer of security is **authentication**. MCP servers should require some form of client identity, typically provided via API keys, bearer tokens, or signed headers. When a `context.initialize` call is made, the server should validate the token associated with the host or the session. This ensures only authorized agents can establish a session or call tools.

```
POST /mcp HTTP/1.1
Authorization: Bearer sk-abc123xyz
Content-Type: application/json
{
  "jsonrpc": "2.0",
  "method": "context.initialize",
  "params": {
    "session_id": "xyz-456",
    "capabilities": { "version": "1.0" }
  },
  "id": 1
}
```

The second layer is **capability scoping and isolation**. Each host should only be able to see and invoke a limited subset of tools, resources, or prompts based on its identity or role. For example, a development agent may access debug-level resources, while a production agent may be restricted to tools labeled `"readonly"`. This scoping is enforced during discovery and invocation. Servers should return method lists that are filtered based on access level, and reject unauthorized calls at runtime with informative errors.

Beyond authentication and access control, **sandboxing** is key. MCP servers should avoid executing arbitrary code or loading host-supplied scripts unless executed in isolated environments like containers, serverless functions, or managed API gateways. If your tool calls an external API or performs file I/O, validate and sanitize all input fields, even if they appear to come from a trusted host.

Trust boundaries must also consider **data sensitivity and auditability**. MCP agents may request access to internal company data, run customer-facing operations, or automate critical infrastructure. Therefore, all tool invocations and resource fetches should be logged in detail—recording the `session_id`, `tool`, `input`, response time, and success/failure. This enables traceability in the event of data leaks, failures, or suspicious behavior.

For production deployments, **rate limiting** and **throttling policies** should also be enforced at the MCP server level. These prevent runaway agents from overloading backend services or incurring unexpected costs, especially when working with third-party APIs or paid compute.

To summarize, secure MCP implementation is not just a feature—it's a necessity. By combining layered authentication, capability scoping, sandboxing, request auditing, and trust-aware architecture, developers can safely extend their AI agents while maintaining strong operational control and minimizing risk.

2.4 From M×N to M+N: Why MCP Is a Scalable Integration Model

One of the most compelling reasons for adopting the Model Context Protocol (MCP) in AI agent architecture is its fundamental shift in integration strategy—from an M×N model to an M+N model. This difference isn't just mathematical—it's architectural. Traditional integrations between AI agents and external tools, APIs, or services often rely on bespoke, one-off connections. Each new tool added to the system must be explicitly wired to each agent that uses it. This leads to M×N complexity, where every agent must be individually connected to every tool. Over time, this results in bloated codebases, unmanageable dependencies, and high maintenance overhead.

MCP changes this paradigm by introducing a decoupled interface where agents (the "M" side) and tools/resources (the "N" side) speak a common language via the protocol. Instead of building point-to-point connections, both ends register and interact through the MCP layer using standardized JSON-RPC method calls. Agents don't need to know implementation details of the tools. They discover them dynamically through `tool.list` or `resource.list`, and invoke them using `tool.invoke` or `resource.fetch`.

Let's illustrate this with a concrete example. Suppose you have three agents: a customer support bot, a financial planning assistant, and an internal IT bot. You also have three services: a CRM API, a financial calculator, and a device provisioning API. In a traditional setup, you might have to hardwire each agent to each service, resulting in 3×3 = 9 separate integrations. With MCP, each of the services implements an MCP-compliant server exposing standard JSON-RPC interfaces, and each agent is just an MCP client. The moment a tool is registered with MCP, all agents can discover it and request invocation, as long as their access permissions allow.

In a working example, the CRM tool might register with the following method schema:

```
{
  "jsonrpc": "2.0",
```

```
  "method": "tool.register",
  "params": {
    "name": "lookup_customer",
    "description": "Get customer profile by email",
    "input_schema": { "type": "object", "properties": {
"email": { "type": "string" } } },
    "output_schema": { "type": "object", "properties": {
"name": { "type": "string" }, "plan": { "type": "string" } }
}
  },
  "id": 1
}
```

Then, when the support bot receives an LLM-generated plan to check customer details, it simply invokes:

```
{
  "jsonrpc": "2.0",
  "method": "tool.invoke",
  "params": {
    "name": "lookup_customer",
    "input": { "email": "alice@example.com" }
  },
  "id": 2
}
```

No need for custom API wrappers or hardcoded business logic. This makes adding a new tool to the ecosystem completely independent of modifying existing agents. Similarly, adding a new agent doesn't require rewriting or duplicating tool logic—it just needs access to the protocol.

The M+N architecture enabled by MCP also allows teams to scale development asynchronously. Tool developers can focus on building reusable services that conform to the protocol, while AI engineers can work on refining agent logic and prompting strategies. The protocol acts as the standardized contract between the two domains, allowing parallel development and faster iteration.

In Summary, MCP's move from M×N to M+N is more than a reduction in integration burden—it's a strategic shift that enables modularity, scalability, and long-term maintainability. For any developer serious about building robust, extensible AI systems, understanding and embracing this shift is a foundational step.

2.5 A Complete MCP Interaction Walkthrough

To truly understand how the Model Context Protocol (MCP) works in practice, it's essential to walk through a complete interaction between an AI agent (client), the MCP host, and an external tool (server). This example demonstrates how MCP standardizes discovery, invocation, and response handling using JSON-RPC 2.0.

Step 1: The Tool Server Registers a Tool

The tool server implements a function and registers it with the MCP host. Here's a Python-based MCP server exposing a simple function that returns weather data for a given city:

```python
# tool_server.py
from mcp_sdk.server import MCPToolServer

server = MCPToolServer()

@server.tool(name="get_weather", description="Fetch current weather for a city")
def get_weather(input: dict) -> dict:
    city = input.get("city")
    return {
        "city": city,
        "temperature": "26° C",
        "condition": "Partly cloudy"
    }

if __name__ == "__main__":
    server.run(port=4000)
```

Once running, this server is discoverable by any MCP-compatible client.

Step 2: The Agent (Client) Discovers the Available Tool

The client (e.g., an AI agent or orchestrator) sends a request to the MCP host to list available tools:

```json
{
  "jsonrpc": "2.0",
  "method": "tool.list",
  "params": {},
  "id": 1
}
```

And receives a response like:

```json
{
  "jsonrpc": "2.0",
  "result": [
    {
      "name": "get_weather",
      "description": "Fetch current weather for a city",
      "input_schema": { "type": "object", "properties": { "city": {
"type": "string" } } }
    }
  ],
  "id": 1
}
```

This response informs the agent that `get_weather` is available and requires a `city` input.

Step 3: The Agent Invokes the Tool via MCP

The agent uses the tool by invoking it through the MCP host:

```json
{
  "jsonrpc": "2.0",
  "method": "tool.invoke",
  "params": {
    "name": "get_weather",
```

```
    "input": {
      "city": "Lagos"
    }
  },
  "id": 2
}
```

The host forwards this request to the `get_weather` server, and returns the response:

```
{
  "jsonrpc": "2.0",
  "result": {
    "city": "Lagos",
    "temperature": "26° C",
    "condition": "Partly cloudy"
  },
  "id": 2
}
```

The agent now has structured, contextual data it can use to continue the conversation, perform calculations, or log into another workflow.

Step 4: Agent Response Construction

The agent formats this result into a natural language reply or inserts it into another process step:

```
llm_prompt = f"The current weather in Lagos is {response['temperature']}
and {response['condition']}."
```

Wrap-Up

This complete interaction illustrates how MCP simplifies tool access and response integration for LLM-powered systems. The separation of responsibilities—registration, discovery, invocation—ensures scalability and modularity. With minimal setup, developers can plug in new tools or swap out backends without changing agent logic. As your agent ecosystem grows, MCP provides the stable backbone to keep your workflows interoperable and maintainable.

Part II – Building with MCP

Chapter 3: Designing MCP Components: Tools, Resources, and Prompts

3.1 MCP Tools: Exposing LLM-Compatible Functions

Exposing functions as tools within the Model Context Protocol (MCP) is one of the most important capabilities for developers building intelligent, modular, and scalable AI agents. Tools represent callable server-side functions—typically small, stateless operations—that an LLM can invoke through the MCP host. The goal is to let LLMs seamlessly query real-time or system-level data, perform actions, or retrieve information that they themselves cannot generate or access.

To define an MCP tool, you'll implement a function on an MCP-compatible server and register it with metadata so that clients (LLM-based agents) can discover and invoke it correctly. A well-designed MCP tool includes a unique name, description, an input schema, and optionally, an output schema for automatic validation.

Let's walk through a complete example using Python and an open-source MCP SDK.

```python
# tool_server.py
from mcp_sdk.server import MCPToolServer

# Create a tool server instance
server = MCPToolServer()

# Define a tool function and register it with MCP
@server.tool(
    name="stock_price_lookup",
    description="Get the current stock price of a given
ticker symbol."
)
def stock_price_lookup(input: dict) -> dict:
    symbol = input.get("symbol", "").upper()
    # Normally, this would call an external API
    if symbol == "AAPL":
        return {"symbol": "AAPL", "price": 185.23}
    elif symbol == "TSLA":
        return {"symbol": "TSLA", "price": 240.17}
```

```
    else:
        return {"error": f"Stock symbol '{symbol}' not
found"}

# Start the server
if __name__ == "__main__":
    server.run(port=5000)
```

In this example, the tool server exposes a single function named
`stock_price_lookup`, which accepts an input dictionary containing a
`symbol` field. It performs a mock lookup and returns structured data. The
decorator `@server.tool` automatically handles JSON-RPC registration and
schema exposure behind the scenes.

Once the server is running, the MCP host will include `stock_price_lookup`
in its registry. Agents can discover it via the `tool.list` method and invoke
it with a `tool.invoke` call, passing `{ "symbol": "AAPL" }` as input. The
response will be a JSON object with the stock price, which the agent can
parse and include in its output reasoning or response generation.

This design makes tools composable, testable, and modular—each tool lives
independently and can evolve separately from the LLM agent logic. As a
result, MCP tools serve as a critical bridge between natural language agents
and operational APIs, enabling richer capabilities without inflating LLM
prompts or hardcoding business logic.

In the next section, we'll explore how MCP resources differ from tools and
how to design them for dynamic, long-context applications.

3.2 MCP Resources: Serving External Contextual Data

In the Model Context Protocol (MCP), **resources** are a distinct mechanism
for exposing structured, static or semi-static data that can be used to enrich
an LLM's prompt with relevant background information. Unlike tools, which
are invoked at runtime like functions, resources serve contextual data in
advance. They are most useful when the agent needs external information to
inform reasoning, generate accurate responses, or maintain long-term
memory—without repeatedly invoking a function call.

31

Resources are defined by their **name**, **description**, and a callable endpoint that returns a JSON-serializable object when queried. These can represent knowledge bases, configurations, summaries, or preprocessed views of real-world systems. Once retrieved by the MCP host, the resource data is embedded in the context window of the LLM or passed into a structured planning layer.

Let's create a simple resource server that exposes product documentation summaries for an internal software tool:

```python
# resource_server.py
from mcp_sdk.server import MCPResourceServer

# Create a resource server instance
server = MCPResourceServer()

# Register a resource endpoint
@server.resource(
    name="devtool_docs",
    description="Summarized documentation for internal
developer tools."
)
def devtool_docs(input: dict) -> dict:
    return {
        "tools": [
            {
                "name": "DevSync",
                "summary": "A CLI tool that syncs development
environments across teams."
            },
            {
                "name": "TestMatrix",
                "summary": "Automates test generation and
coverage analytics for CI/CD pipelines."
            }
        ]
    }

# Start the resource server
if __name__ == "__main__":
    server.run(port=7000)
```

Once this resource server is running, it can be queried by the MCP host using the standard `resource.get` method. When a developer-facing LLM agent starts a session—say, one embedded into an IDE or an internal Slack bot—the host can preload this documentation resource into the agent's prompt like this:

```
{
  "resources": {
    "devtool_docs": {
      "tools": [
        {
          "name": "DevSync",
          "summary": "A CLI tool that syncs development
environments across teams."
        },
        {
          "name": "TestMatrix",
          "summary": "Automates test generation and coverage
analytics for CI/CD pipelines."
        }
      ]
    }
  }
}
```

The agent then uses this structured context to answer developer questions more intelligently, such as "What tool should I use to ensure test coverage?" or "Can I sync my team's local env with a CLI?"

The key benefit of resources is that they decouple LLM context from computation. You preload data that doesn't need to change on every call, but is still vital for accurate responses. This leads to improved latency, reduced token usage, and more stable prompt design. In later chapters, we'll explore how to persist resources, manage updates efficiently, and combine them with tools and prompts to power sophisticated, intelligent workflows.

3.3 Crafting Effective Prompts: Templates for Reuse

In the Model Context Protocol (MCP), **prompts** serve as the final stage of context injection before an LLM produces its response. While tools and resources provide dynamic and static data respectively, prompts define how that data is **framed, structured, and delivered** to the model. The use of

template-based prompts ensures consistency, reusability, and clarity across different tasks and agent interactions. This section focuses on how developers can craft and register effective prompt templates within an MCP-based system.

A prompt in MCP is typically a string or message template with placeholders for contextual variables. These placeholders are filled at runtime using data from resources, tool outputs, or user input. Well-designed prompts reduce ambiguity, guide model behavior, and increase accuracy—especially when used with structured agents that rely on predictable context patterns.

Let's walk through a hands-on example of defining and using a prompt template in a coding assistant scenario.

First, define the reusable prompt using a Python-compatible templating style:

```python
# prompt_templates.py

prompt_templates = {
    "code_review": {
        "description": "Prompt template for reviewing a code snippet with suggestions.",
        "template": (
            "You are an expert software engineer.\n"
            "Please review the following code and provide suggestions for improvement:\n"
            "{code_block}\n"
            "Be concise, focus on correctness, performance, and readability."
        )
    },
    "bug_explanation": {
        "description": "Explain what the code below does and identify potential bugs.",
        "template": (
            "Analyze the following code:\n"
            "{code_block}\n"
            "Explain what it does, and highlight any logical errors or edge cases it may miss."
        )
    }
}
```

Now imagine a user submits a code snippet. The MCP host retrieves the appropriate template, injects the snippet into the placeholder, and sends the final prompt to the LLM:

```python
def render_prompt(template_name, variables):
    base = prompt_templates[template_name]["template"]
    return base.format(**variables)

# Example usage
user_code = """
def divide(a, b):
    return a / b
"""

final_prompt = render_prompt("bug_explanation",
{"code_block": user_code})
print(final_prompt)
```

The result:

```
Analyze the following code:
def divide(a, b):
    return a / b

Explain what it does, and highlight any logical errors or
edge cases it may miss.
```

This formatted prompt is now passed to the LLM as part of the `invoke` call via the MCP host. Because it's reusable and modular, the same template can be applied across multiple use cases—chatbot interfaces, voice assistants, IDE agents, or even batch jobs.

Prompt templates become even more powerful when stored alongside metadata like version tags, categories, or tags for tracking which ones perform best under which conditions. In more advanced use cases, prompts can be stored in version-controlled registries or retrieved dynamically based on agent type or user persona.

In short, crafting high-quality, reusable prompts is not an afterthought—it's a core pillar of any MCP-powered AI system. Standardizing your prompt architecture early on will lead to more robust agents, simpler debugging, and consistent user experiences across tools.

35

3.4 Designing for Reusability and Modularity

In MCP-based systems, designing for reusability and modularity isn't just good practice—it's a necessity for maintaining scalable, adaptable, and maintainable AI agents. Since agents often rely on combinations of tools, resources, and prompts to function, your architecture must be composable by default. This section focuses on how to structure MCP components so they can be reused across tasks, chained into workflows, and versioned independently.

To begin with, each MCP component—whether a tool (a function the agent can call), a resource (a data provider), or a prompt (a template to guide output)—should follow a **single-responsibility principle**. That means every component should be built to solve one well-defined problem. For example, don't combine user authentication and user analytics into one tool. Split them into `auth.validate_user` and `analytics.log_user_action`.

In Python, you can organize tools in a modular package:

```python
# tools/auth.py
def validate_user(email: str, password: str) -> bool:
    # Authentication logic
    return email == "admin@example.com" and password ==
"secure"

# tools/analytics.py
def log_user_action(user_id: str, action: str):
    # Send event to tracking DB or message queue
    print(f"User {user_id} performed action: {action}")
```

Each tool is now independently testable, importable, and callable via MCP JSON-RPC methods such as `auth.validate_user` and `analytics.log_user_action`.

For resources, modularity means encapsulating data-fetching logic into endpoints that can be recombined and cached. Example:

```python
# resources/user_profile.py
def get_user_profile(user_id: str) -> dict:
    return {
```

```
        "user_id": user_id,
        "name": "Jane Doe",
        "plan": "pro",
        "features": ["chatbot", "analytics"]
    }
```

This resource can be reused in many contexts—whether customizing UI, constructing LLM prompts, or personalizing tool responses.

Now consider a modular prompt registry:

```
# prompts/templates.py
prompt_templates = {
    "greet_user": "Hello {name}, how can I assist you
today?",
    "plan_info": "You're currently on the {plan} plan, which
includes: {features}."
}
```

By separating your logic and keeping templates in centralized, parameterized definitions, you enable full **reuse** across teams, apps, and agents. Each prompt becomes a reusable contract with variable inputs.

The real power of this design becomes evident when you compose these modules dynamically:

```
from tools.auth import validate_user
from resources.user_profile import get_user_profile
from prompts.templates import prompt_templates

def generate_personalized_intro(user_id):
    profile = get_user_profile(user_id)
    return prompt_templates["plan_info"].format(**profile)

print(generate_personalized_intro("12345"))
```

Because tools, resources, and prompts are modular, you can test, mock, reuse, and update them in isolation. This improves velocity, reduces bugs, and enables version control across your MCP ecosystem.

In , reusability and modularity allow MCP developers to build systems that are flexible, testable, and easy to scale. Treat every function, resource, and prompt as a composable unit—just like microservices in traditional backend development. It's not just about writing clean code; it's about building AI agents that can evolve over time.

3.5 Combining Tools, Resources, and Prompts for Complex Workflows

Combining tools, resources, and prompts is where the real power of MCP unfolds—this is how you create intelligent, context-aware agents that can operate across diverse tasks, adapt to user input, and interact with systems in real time. Rather than thinking of tools, resources, and prompts as isolated pieces, you should design them as interoperable components of a pipeline that can be orchestrated to perform complex workflows end-to-end.

Let's start with a scenario: imagine you're building a support agent that helps users troubleshoot software issues, upsell them to higher-tier plans if needed, and generate a report of the interaction. In this workflow, the agent must (1) authenticate the user, (2) fetch user profile data, (3) craft appropriate messages based on their current subscription, (4) guide them through troubleshooting steps using LLM calls, and (5) log the final outcome.

Each of these steps aligns with an MCP component:

- **Tools** handle actions such as `auth.verify_token`, `support.run_diagnostics`, and `billing.upgrade_plan`.
- **Resources** expose structured data like `user.get_profile`, `support.faq`, or `plans.get_available_upgrades`.
- **Prompts** define how the LLM should respond given the user state and context—e.g., "If the user is on a basic plan and has frequent issues, recommend upgrade."

Here's how you wire these together in a real implementation using MCP's JSON-RPC format and Python handler stubs:

```python
# tools/auth.py
def verify_token(token: str) -> dict:
    # Validate token and return user ID
    return {"user_id": "u-12345"}

# resources/user.py
def get_profile(user_id: str) -> dict:
```

```
        return {"user_id": user_id, "plan": "basic",
"issues_last_month": 5}

# tools/support.py
def run_diagnostics(user_id: str) -> dict:
        return {"status": "intermittent failures detected"}

# prompts/templates.py
prompt_templates = {
    "recommend_upgrade": (
        "The user is on the {plan} plan and has reported
{issues_last_month} issues. "
        "Suggest a relevant upgrade and explain the
benefits."
    )
}
```

Now let's simulate the agent behavior:

```
# mcp_orchestrator.py
from tools.auth import verify_token
from resources.user import get_profile
from tools.support import run_diagnostics
from prompts.templates import prompt_templates

def handle_support_session(token: str):
    user = verify_token(token)
    profile = get_profile(user["user_id"])
    diag = run_diagnostics(user["user_id"])

    prompt =
prompt_templates["recommend_upgrade"].format(**profile)
    llm_response = call_llm(prompt)   # hypothetical LLM
function call
    return {
        "diagnostics": diag,
        "llm_recommendation": llm_response
    }

print(handle_support_session("sample.jwt.token"))
```

This is an MCP-aligned, hands-on implementation. You define JSON-RPC
methods that represent tools and resources, then use those methods to gather
input context and feed structured prompts to an LLM. The orchestration

logic—what ties everything together—can reside in the client application, or even inside a meta-agent capable of chaining tools and resources autonomously.

You'll find this architecture scales well: new workflows simply recombine existing tools and resources. For example, you could extend the same setup to trigger billing APIs or notify support staff via Slack with minimal code duplication.

To wrap up: combining tools, resources, and prompts transforms your MCP implementation from isolated RPC calls into intelligent, stateful workflows. When structured properly, this approach supports everything from chatbots to autonomous agents with reliable, interpretable, and evolvable behavior. The key is consistency—use well-defined schemas, standardized method names, and predictable prompt templates so your agents remain modular, traceable, and production-grade.

Chapter 4: Building an MCP Server from Scratch

4.1 Project Setup, Environment, and MCP SDK Basics

Building an MCP server from scratch begins with setting up a clean, minimal project structure and integrating the MCP SDK to expose callable tools and resources via JSON-RPC. Your server will function as a provider of context—structured data, functions, or prompts—that LLM-based agents can invoke remotely during conversations or workflows. This section walks through setting up a complete development environment, initializing the project layout, and wiring up your first MCP-compliant endpoint using Python.

Start by creating a new project directory and initializing a Python environment:

```
mkdir mcp_server
cd mcp_server
python -m venv venv
source venv/bin/activate   # On Windows use
venv\Scripts\activate
pip install fastapi uvicorn pydantic
```

Although MCP implementations are protocol-agnostic, we'll use FastAPI here to handle JSON-RPC over HTTP. Now structure your project like this:

```
mcp_server/
├── server.py
├── tools/
│   └── math_tools.py
├── resources/
│   └── docs.py
├── schemas/
│   └── __init__.py
└── prompts/
    └── templates.py
```

Now let's create a simple tool: a math function that adds two numbers. This will be exposed over JSON-RPC.

```python
# tools/math_tools.py
def add_numbers(a: int, b: int) -> dict:
    result = a + b
    return {"result": result}
```

Next, implement the server using FastAPI with a basic JSON-RPC dispatcher:

```python
# server.py
from fastapi import FastAPI, Request
from tools.math_tools import add_numbers

app = FastAPI()

@app.post("/rpc")
async def json_rpc_endpoint(request: Request):
    body = await request.json()
    method = body.get("method")
    params = body.get("params", {})
    id_ = body.get("id")

    if method == "math.add":
        result = add_numbers(**params)
    else:
        result = {"error": f"Unknown method {method}"}

    return {
        "jsonrpc": "2.0",
        "result": result,
        "id": id_
    }
```

Launch the server with:

```
uvicorn server:app --reload
```

Now, simulate a client call using `curl`:

```
curl -X POST http://localhost:8000/rpc \
  -H "Content-Type: application/json" \
```

```
  -d '{"jsonrpc": "2.0", "method": "math.add", "params":
{"a": 4, "b": 7}, "id": 1}'
```

You should receive:

```
{
  "jsonrpc": "2.0",
  "result": {"result": 11},
  "id": 1
}
```

This simple tool demonstrates the entire JSON-RPC handshake expected by any MCP-compatible client or agent. From here, you can add more complex tools, serve structured data as resources, and later apply prompt logic to dynamically shape LLM output.

In summary, setting up your MCP server from scratch is a matter of establishing clear project scaffolding, implementing callable tools and resources as methods, and exposing them through a lightweight JSON-RPC server. This foundation supports scalable, interoperable integration with client-side agents, and sets the stage for chaining, orchestration, and advanced context management later in the book.

4.2 Implementing Tools (Function Endpoints) with Real Code

Implementing tools in an MCP server means creating function endpoints that your LLM agents can invoke via JSON-RPC. These tools perform atomic tasks—anything from arithmetic operations to external API calls—and return structured results. In MCP terms, a "tool" is simply a callable, semantically named function that's discoverable by clients and used during prompt execution or agent reasoning.

Let's walk through implementing such a tool with complete working code.

Step 1: Define the Tool Logic

Let's create a tool that queries the current weather using a mock service. You'll organize it in the `tools/weather_tools.py` file.

```
# tools/weather_tools.py

from typing import Dict

def get_weather(city: str) -> Dict:
    # In production, this would query a real API like OpenWeatherMap
    mock_weather_data = {
        "New York": {"temp": 23, "condition": "Clear"},
        "London": {"temp": 18, "condition": "Cloudy"},
        "Tokyo": {"temp": 26, "condition": "Rainy"}
    }

    data = mock_weather_data.get(city, {"temp": None, "condition":
"Unknown"})
    return {
        "city": city,
        "temperature": data["temp"],
        "condition": data["condition"]
    }
```

This mock returns data for a few cities. In a real tool, you'd fetch this data from a live API and handle request timeouts, API keys, and retries. But the key structure—input, processing, return—is preserved.

Step 2: Expose the Tool in the Server

Update your FastAPI JSON-RPC dispatcher in `server.py` to route this tool.

```
# server.py (add import)
from tools.weather_tools import get_weather

@app.post("/rpc")
async def json_rpc_endpoint(request: Request):
    body = await request.json()
    method = body.get("method")
    params = body.get("params", {})
    id_ = body.get("id")

    if method == "math.add":
```

```
        result = add_numbers(**params)
    elif method == "weather.get":
        result = get_weather(**params)
    else:
        result = {"error": f"Unknown method {method}"}


    return {
        "jsonrpc": "2.0",
        "result": result,
        "id": id_
    }
```

Step 3: Test the Tool

Use `curl` to simulate a client calling the tool:

```
curl -X POST http://localhost:8000/rpc \
  -H "Content-Type: application/json" \
  -d '{"jsonrpc": "2.0", "method": "weather.get", "params": {"city":
"London"}, "id": 2}'
```

Expected output:

```
{
  "jsonrpc": "2.0",
  "result": {
    "city": "London",
    "temperature": 18,
    "condition": "Cloudy"
  },
  "id": 2
}
```

Optional: Add Schema Validation

To make your tool more robust, you can define parameter and return types
using `pydantic`:

```
# schemas/weather.py
```

```
from pydantic import BaseModel

class WeatherParams(BaseModel):
    city: str
```

Then in `server.py`:

```
from schemas.weather import WeatherParams

elif method == "weather.get":
    validated = WeatherParams(**params)
    result = get_weather(validated.city)
```

Wrap-up

This section has walked you through defining, exposing, and testing an
MCP-compliant tool. Every tool should follow this structure: accept typed
input, perform a specific task, and return clean, JSON-serializable output.
These tools form the building blocks of AI agent capability, allowing LLMs
to invoke external functionality securely and scalably using MCP as a
universal interface.

4.3 Exposing Resources (Data Providers) with Examples

In the MCP (Model Context Protocol) ecosystem, **Resources** are structured
data providers that supply external context to AI agents. While Tools are
functions the agent can call, Resources are *datasets or endpoints the agent
can read from*, typically at the start of a session or as background context.
These resources often include JSON payloads fetched by MCP Hosts or
Clients and injected into the agent's prompt, memory, or internal state.

Let's build and expose an MCP Resource step-by-step using a real example.

Step 1: Understand the Resource Pattern

Resources should be served as JSON endpoints on your MCP Server, following predictable paths. They are invoked using the MCP method namespace `resource.{resource_name}` and return structured dictionaries or lists—ideally with consistent keys.

Let's say you want to expose a resource called `company.knowledgebase`, which returns a list of recent policy updates or FAQs.

Step 2: Create the Resource Logic

Create a file named `resources/company_knowledge.py` with the following logic:

```python
# resources/company_knowledge.py

from typing import List, Dict

def get_knowledgebase() -> List[Dict]:
    return [
        {
            "title": "Remote Work Policy",
            "updated": "2025-06-01",
            "content": "All employees may work remotely up to three days
a week."
        },
        {
            "title": "Expense Reimbursement",
            "updated": "2025-05-15",
            "content": "Receipts must be submitted within 30 days of
travel."
        },
        {
            "title": "Security Update",
            "updated": "2025-05-10",
            "content": "All systems now require two-factor
authentication."
        }
```

```
        ]
```

This resource returns a static list of objects, simulating a backend fetch from a company's internal knowledge database.

Step 3: Expose the Resource via the MCP Server

Update your MCP server's JSON-RPC dispatcher to handle this resource:

```python
# server.py (add import)
from resources.company_knowledge import get_knowledgebase


@app.post("/rpc")
async def json_rpc_endpoint(request: Request):
    body = await request.json()
    method = body.get("method")
    params = body.get("params", {})
    id_ = body.get("id")

    if method == "resource.company.knowledgebase":
        result = get_knowledgebase()
    # existing tool handlers here...
    else:
        result = {"error": f"Unknown method {method}"}

    return {
        "jsonrpc": "2.0",
        "result": result,
        "id": id_
    }
```

Step 4: Test the Resource

To simulate an MCP client requesting this context:

```
curl -X POST http://localhost:8000/rpc ¥
  -H "Content-Type: application/json" ¥
  -d '{"jsonrpc": "2.0", "method": "resource.company.knowledgebase",
"id": 3}'
```

Expected output:

```
{
  "jsonrpc": "2.0",
  "result": [
    {
      "title": "Remote Work Policy",
      "updated": "2025-06-01",
      "content": "All employees may work remotely up to three days a
week."
    },
    {
      "title": "Expense Reimbursement",
      "updated": "2025-05-15",
      "content": "Receipts must be submitted within 30 days of travel."
    },
    {
      "title": "Security Update",
      "updated": "2025-05-10",
      "content": "All systems now require two-factor authentication."
    }
  ],
  "id": 3
}
```

This response is context-ready—an LLM agent can ingest it at runtime to better answer questions like, "What's the latest remote work policy?"

Optional: Add Dynamic Behavior

To make the resource respond to parameters (e.g. department: "HR"), simply accept params and filter accordingly:

49

```
def get_knowledgebase(department: str = None) -> List[Dict]:
    # Filter logic here (not shown)
    ...
```

Update the JSON-RPC handler to parse parameters and pass them to the resource.

Wrap-up

Resources in MCP are critical for grounding agent decisions with real-time, structured data. They're declarative, context-first, and often session-aware. By exposing a well-designed `resource.*` interface, you allow your agents to operate as if they were contextually embedded in your backend systems— without tightly coupling the AI logic to the data layer.

This practice ensures separation of concerns, promotes interoperability, and accelerates the development of context-rich agent workflows.

4.4 Local Debugging, Output Inspection, and Error Fixes

In MCP development, robust local debugging is non-negotiable. Whether you're exposing a Tool or Resource, you must validate that your server responds correctly, handles unexpected input gracefully, and returns agent-ready JSON. Local debugging not only speeds up iteration but helps catch integration failures before they escalate into confusing agent-side behavior. In this section, we'll walk through how to set up a controlled debugging workflow using a minimal server and structured test calls.

Let's assume you've already implemented a basic MCP server exposing both a Tool (`tool.math.add`) and a Resource (`resource.company.knowledgebase`). Your goal now is to inspect request/response cycles, handle malformed input, and verify that all returned payloads are JSON-serializable and prompt-safe.

Step 1: Run the Server Locally with Debug Logging

Use a local development server such as **Uvicorn** with hot-reload and detailed logging enabled. In your project root, run:

```
uvicorn server:app --reload --port 8000 --log-level debug
```

This gives you visibility into every incoming request, headers, and JSON body, which is crucial for catching method name mismatches or parameter errors.

Step 2: Simulate JSON-RPC Requests with `curl` or `httpie`

Use `curl` or `httpie` to manually send JSON-RPC requests. For example, test a correct call:

```
curl -X POST http://localhost:8000/rpc ¥
  -H "Content-Type: application/json" ¥
  -d ' {"jsonrpc": "2.0", "method": "tool.math.add", "params": {"a": 4, "b": 7}, "id": 1}'
```

You should receive:

```
{
  "jsonrpc": "2.0",
  "result": 11,
  "id": 1
}
Now test an invalid one to simulate an error:
curl -X POST http://localhost:8000/rpc \
  -H "Content-Type: application/json" \
  -d '{"jsonrpc": "2.0", "method": "tool.math.add", "params":
{"a": 4}, "id": 2}'
```

Expected output:

```
{
  "jsonrpc": "2.0",
  "error": {
    "code": -32602,
```

```
      "message": "Missing required parameter: 'b'"
   },
   "id": 2
}
```

This is an opportunity to implement better error handling in your tool logic.

Step 3: Add Robust Error Messages and Stack Trace Logging

Update your endpoint handler in `server.py` to catch exceptions and provide developer-friendly feedback:

```python
@app.post("/rpc")
async def json_rpc_endpoint(request: Request):
    try:
        body = await request.json()
        method = body.get("method")
        params = body.get("params", {})
        id_ = body.get("id")

        if method == "tool.math.add":
            result = math_add(**params)
        elif method == "resource.company.knowledgebase":
            result = get_knowledgebase()
        else:
            raise ValueError(f"Unknown method '{method}'")

        return {"jsonrpc": "2.0", "result": result, "id": id_}

    except Exception as e:
        import traceback
        traceback.print_exc()
        return {
            "jsonrpc": "2.0",
            "error": {
                "code": -32603,
                "message": str(e)
```

```
        },
        "id": id_
    }
```

This outputs detailed stack traces to your console, while keeping the response client-safe.

Step 4: Inspect Outputs for Prompt Injection and Serialization Issues

Use `json.dumps(result, indent=2)` in your debug logs to inspect large payloads like resource data. Validate that:

- All data is JSON-serializable.
- There are no embedded functions or objects (like datetime without formatting).
- Strings are prompt-safe and avoid shell code, special characters, or sensitive metadata.

For example:

```
import json
print(json.dumps(result, indent=2))
```

This helps ensure that what you're returning is truly ready for agent prompting or summarization.

Step 5: Build a Local Test Script

Rather than running `curl` manually each time, create a Python script:

```
# test_client.py
import requests

payload = {
    "jsonrpc": "2.0",
```

```
    "method": "tool.math.add",
    "params": {"a": 10, "b": 5},
    "id": 1
}

resp = requests.post("http://localhost:8000/rpc", json=payload)
print(resp.json())
```

Run this repeatedly as you refine the tool behavior.

Wrap-up

Local debugging is your safety net when building with MCP. Always test each tool and resource endpoint with real JSON-RPC calls, validate against malformed input, and inspect your logs for unexpected behavior. Good debugging isn't just about fixing errors—it's about building confidence that what your server sends is what your agent expects. Once this local layer is solid, production readiness becomes much easier to achieve.

4.5 Securing Your Server

Securing your MCP server is a non-negotiable requirement when deploying tools and resources that interact with LLM agents, especially in production environments. At its core, security involves two critical layers: **authentication** (verifying who is calling the server) and **input validation** (ensuring the data received is safe and expected). Without both, your server becomes vulnerable to unauthorized access, prompt injection, data leaks, or unexpected execution behavior.

Let's begin by adding **authentication using bearer tokens**. This is one of the most common and effective patterns for authorizing client requests. When your agent or orchestrator sends a JSON-RPC call to your MCP server, it must include an `Authorization` header with a secure token. Your server verifies the token before processing the request.

Here's how to enforce that pattern in a FastAPI-based MCP server:

```
from fastapi import FastAPI, Request, HTTPException

app = FastAPI()
AUTH_TOKEN = "your-secure-token"

@app.post("/rpc")
async def json_rpc(request: Request):
    auth = request.headers.get("Authorization")
    if auth != f"Bearer {AUTH_TOKEN}":
        raise HTTPException(status_code=401,
detail="Unauthorized")

    payload = await request.json()
    # Process payload as normal
```

You can store the token securely using environment variables and load them using os.environ, rather than hardcoding. This ensures the token can be rotated without redeploying code.

Now let's move to **input validation**, which is especially important when working with LLM-facing tools. If your tool expects a and b as integers, but the agent sends malformed data (either by accident or maliciously), your server should fail gracefully.

Use Pydantic models for structured validation. Here's how you could validate a math tool input:

```
from pydantic import BaseModel, ValidationError
from fastapi import Body

class AddParams(BaseModel):
    a: int
    b: int

@app.post("/rpc")
async def json_rpc(request: Request):
    auth = request.headers.get("Authorization")
    if auth != f"Bearer {AUTH_TOKEN}":
        raise HTTPException(status_code=401,
detail="Unauthorized")

    try:
        body = await request.json()
```

```
        method = body.get("method")
        params = body.get("params", {})
        id_ = body.get("id")

        if method == "tool.math.add":
            parsed = AddParams(**params)
            result = parsed.a + parsed.b
        else:
            raise ValueError("Unknown method")

        return {"jsonrpc": "2.0", "result": result, "id":
id_}

    except ValidationError as ve:
        return {
            "jsonrpc": "2.0",
            "error": {"code": -32602, "message": "Invalid
parameters", "data": ve.errors()},
            "id": body.get("id", None)
        }
    except Exception as e:
        return {
            "jsonrpc": "2.0",
            "error": {"code": -32603, "message": str(e)},
            "id": body.get("id", None)
        }
```

This way, your server guarantees that all incoming requests are both **authorized** and **validated** before any computation or resource lookup is performed.

Finally, consider rate-limiting and IP restrictions as an added defense, especially if your MCP server will be exposed to the internet. You can implement these using reverse proxies (e.g., NGINX with fail2ban), API gateways, or frameworks like `slowapi` for FastAPI.

In summary, a secure MCP server enforces strict bearer token authentication, validates every payload using typed schemas, and rejects malformed or unauthorized requests immediately. This forms the foundation for safe and reliable agent interaction in real-world AI systems.

Chapter 5: MCP Clients – Integrating LLM Apps with MCP

5.1 Installing and Using the MCP Client Libraries

To integrate your AI application with MCP as a client, the first step is to install and initialize the MCP client libraries. These libraries abstract away the low-level JSON-RPC handling and make it straightforward to interact with MCP-compliant servers, tools, and resources. Whether you're building an LLM-based chatbot, automation assistant, or intelligent agent pipeline, the MCP client serves as the bridge between your application and the broader context-aware ecosystem.

To get started, install the `mcp-sdk` client library using pip. This package provides utilities to send JSON-RPC requests to an MCP server, manage tool/resource calls, and handle responses.

```
pip install mcp-sdk
```

After installation, you can initialize a basic client in Python using the SDK's `MCPClient` class. Below is a practical example where a client connects to an MCP server and invokes a simple math tool that adds two numbers. This assumes the server exposes a tool with the method name `tool.math.add`.

```python
from mcp_sdk import MCPClient

# Initialize the MCP client with the server URL and
authentication token
client = MCPClient(
    url="http://localhost:8000/rpc",
    auth_token="your-secure-token"
)

# Call a registered tool
response = client.call_tool(
    method="tool.math.add",
    params={"a": 10, "b": 5}
)
```

```
# Print the result
print(response.result)    # Output: 15
```

Behind the scenes, the `call_tool` method formats the JSON-RPC request, sends it to the server, attaches your bearer token, and parses the result. If the server returns an error, the SDK will expose it through the `response.error` property, allowing you to handle failures gracefully in your client logic.

Additionally, the SDK supports setting timeouts, custom headers, and retry policies. You can configure these when creating the `MCPClient` instance to match the reliability and latency requirements of your application.

Here's an example using advanced options:

```
client = MCPClient(
    url="https://my-mcp-server.com/rpc",
    auth_token="prod-token-xyz",
    timeout=5.0,    # in seconds
    retries=3       # retry failed calls up to 3 times
)
```

Once your client is working, you can start chaining multiple tool calls, accessing data resources, and integrating responses into your prompt templates. This setup enables seamless real-time context enrichment for any LLM app without hard-coding logic or duplicating functionality.

To summarize, installing and using the MCP client library is the first foundational step to integrating external tools and resources into your LLM-based application. The SDK handles all the heavy lifting—authentication, formatting, and response parsing—so you can focus on building smart, extensible agents powered by modular server capabilities.

5.2 Connecting to Remote MCP Servers in Code

Integrating with a remote MCP server involves securely establishing a connection from your client application to a live server endpoint that exposes tools and resources over JSON-RPC. This step allows your AI agent to retrieve real-time data, call external tools, or enrich its reasoning using context from third-party systems—without bundling all logic locally. The core of this process is handled by the `MCPClient`, which communicates over HTTP using standard JSON-RPC 2.0 messages.

To demonstrate this in practice, let's assume you're building an LLM-powered assistant that needs to connect to a production MCP server hosted at `https://api.yourdomain.com/mcp`. The server exposes a tool named `tool.weather.get_forecast`, and it requires a secure bearer token for authentication.

First, you install the required package, if you haven't already:

```
pip install mcp-sdk
```

Next, configure the `MCPClient` instance to point to your remote MCP server. It's important to pass a valid authentication token, ideally stored securely via environment variables or a secrets manager.

```python
import os
from mcp_sdk import MCPClient

# Load auth token securely from environment
auth_token = os.getenv("MCP_AUTH_TOKEN")

# Initialize the client to point to the remote MCP server
client = MCPClient(
    url="https://api.yourdomain.com/mcp",
    auth_token=auth_token,
    timeout=10.0,  # Optional: timeout in seconds
    retries=2      # Optional: retry failed requests
)
```

Once connected, you can start invoking server-side tools. For example, let's call the `tool.weather.get_forecast` method to get a 5-day forecast for Lagos:

```python
response = client.call_tool(
    method="tool.weather.get_forecast",
    params={"location": "Lagos", "days": 5}
)

# Check and use the result
if response.error:
```

```
    print("MCP Error:", response.error)
else:
    forecast = response.result
    print("5-day forecast:", forecast)
```

This will return structured weather data that you can directly embed into LLM prompts or downstream decisions. Behind the scenes, the client handles the JSON-RPC 2.0 request format, attaches your token to the `Authorization` header, and parses the server's response.

When working in production environments, it's also essential to verify SSL certificates, use request timeouts, and handle intermittent network failures gracefully. The `MCPClient` allows these configurations via its constructor, and you can extend its behavior if needed.

To summarize, connecting to a remote MCP server from your application is a straightforward yet powerful step. By securely configuring your `MCPClient` instance with the right endpoint and credentials, you unlock the ability to offload logic to dynamic, scalable backend tools—all while maintaining a clean, modular architecture in your AI application. This is the bridge between your LLM's reasoning and real-world, dynamic context.

5.3 Injecting Real-Time Context into Prompts via Resources

Injecting real-time context into prompts via MCP resources is one of the most powerful ways to enhance the performance and relevance of an LLM application. Instead of relying solely on the static information in a model's context window, you can dynamically pull in fresh data from your MCP server—news, weather, pricing, inventory, or any structured domain-specific source—and weave it directly into your prompt construction. This enables your AI agent to stay grounded in facts, react to change, and deliver accurate, up-to-date responses.

Let's walk through a hands-on example where your LLM client app retrieves contextual data from an MCP resource endpoint and uses that data to compose a prompt. Suppose your MCP server exposes a resource called `resource.company.stock_price` that returns real-time stock prices for any given ticker symbol.

First, configure the MCP client as shown previously:

61

```
from mcp_sdk import MCPClient

client = MCPClient(
    url="https://api.yourdomain.com/mcp",
    auth_token="YOUR_BEARER_TOKEN"
)
```

Now, make a call to the resource to fetch the current stock price of a company like Tesla (TSLA):

```
stock_data = client.call_resource(
    method="resource.company.stock_price",
    params={"symbol": "TSLA"}
)

if stock_data.error:
    print("Error fetching stock data:", stock_data.error)
else:
    tsla_price = stock_data.result.get("price")
    print("Current TSLA stock price:", tsla_price)
```

Assume the MCP server returns:

```
{ "symbol": "TSLA", "price": 255.30, "currency": "USD" }
```

With this result, you can now construct a prompt that injects this live context into a question for the LLM:

```
user_query = "Is now a good time to invest in Tesla?"
prompt = f"""You are a financial assistant with access to
real-time stock data.
The current price of TSLA is ${tsla_price} USD.
Based on this and general market conditions, respond to the
user's question:

Question: {user_query}
Answer:"""

# Send to your LLM
response = your_llm.call(prompt)
print(response)
```

In this flow, the MCP resource serves as the authoritative data layer, and your prompt becomes dynamically generated per request. This makes the system more adaptable, prevents hallucination, and grounds the model in verifiable information.

In production, it's important to implement guardrails. Always check for `None` or missing values in the response, and fall back to template defaults or warning messages when the MCP resource fails. You can also cache resource results to improve performance or reduce load during bursts.

In summary, by injecting data from MCP resources into prompts at runtime, you're not just enhancing your AI's answers—you're enabling true contextual awareness. This pattern transforms LLM applications from generic responders into intelligent, data-driven assistants that reflect the current state of the world.

5.4 Handling Failures, Timeouts, and Invalid Outputs

When integrating LLM applications with MCP, robust error handling becomes essential for reliability and user trust. Failures can occur at multiple levels: the MCP server may be unreachable, a specific tool or resource might raise an internal error, or the returned data may be malformed or invalid. Your client logic must be equipped to gracefully detect, manage, and recover from these scenarios without compromising the user experience or the integrity of the AI's response.

Let's start with a basic MCP client call and then expand it to handle timeouts, invalid responses, and fallback behavior. Suppose you're querying an MCP resource named `resource.weather.current`.

Step 1: Setup the MCP Client

```
from mcp_sdk import MCPClient, MCPError
import requests

client = MCPClient(
    url="https://api.example.com/mcp",
    auth_token="your_api_key_here",
    timeout=5  # seconds
)
```

Here, the `timeout` ensures that your call doesn't hang indefinitely waiting for a response.

Step 2: Perform the Call with Error Handling

```python
def get_weather(city):
    try:
        response = client.call_resource(
            method="resource.weather.current",
            params={"location": city}
        )

        if response.error:
            print("MCP returned an error:", response.error)
            return f"⚠️ Could not fetch weather data for {city}."

        data = response.result
        if "temperature" not in data or "condition" not in data:
            raise ValueError("Incomplete weather data received")

        temp = data["temperature"]
        condition = data["condition"]
        return f"The current weather in {city} is {temp}° C and
{condition}."

    except MCPError as mcp_err:
        print("MCP-level error:", mcp_err)
        return f"❌ MCP service is temporarily unavailable."

    except requests.exceptions.Timeout:
        print("Request timed out.")
        return f"⏰ Weather request timed out for {city}. Try again
shortly."

    except Exception as e:
        print("Unexpected error:", str(e))
        return f"🚫 An unexpected error occurred while fetching weather
for {city}."
```

Step 3: Using It in an LLM Prompt

Once you have the response or fallback string, inject it into your prompt:

```
weather_summary = get_weather("Sydney")


prompt = f"""You are a travel assistant.
Here's the real-time weather data to help answer user questions:


{weather_summary}


User: Should I pack light clothes for Sydney?
Assistant:"""
```

Considerations for Robustness

- **Timeouts and retries:** If you encounter transient issues like timeouts or 5xx errors, implement a retry strategy using `backoff` or `tenacity`.
- **Output validation:** Always validate response fields before injecting them into prompts. Don't assume structure—enforce it.
- **Fallback mechanisms:** Predefine friendly fallback responses so your agent doesn't hallucinate or return technical errors to the user.
- **Monitoring:** Log every failure path, including timeouts, malformed payloads, and retries. This makes debugging and operations easier.

Wrap-Up

Handling failures, timeouts, and invalid outputs isn't just about defensive programming—it's a core design responsibility when building production-ready AI systems with MCP. Your agent must be resilient, predictable, and secure even when upstream services misbehave. Treat every MCP call as an external dependency that might fail—and ensure your system is always ready to continue functioning without collapsing the entire flow.

5.5 Real Project: Building an AI Chatbot with MCP Capabilities

To build a production-ready AI chatbot with MCP capabilities, you'll wire up a live connection between your LLM-powered frontend and a backend MCP server exposing tools and contextual resources. The chatbot will dynamically call functions, fetch real-time data, and inject responses into prompts using MCP's JSON-RPC interface. This section walks you through every piece of the puzzle—from architecture to working code—so that by the end, you have a functional, extensible chatbot with real-world usefulness.

Step 1: Project Structure and Setup

Let's begin by organizing the project folder:

```
ai_chatbot_mcp/
├──── client/
│      ├──── main.py
│      └──── mcp_client.py
├──── server/
│      ├──── tools.py
│      └──── resources.py
├──── requirements.txt
```

Your environment must have the following installed:

```
pip install fastapi uvicorn openai mcp-sdk
```

For this example, we assume you've deployed an MCP server that exposes two components:

- `tool.get_weather` – a tool that fetches weather data
- `resource.user_profile` – a resource that retrieves user-specific preferences

Step 2: MCP Client Logic (`mcp_client.py`)

```
from mcp_sdk import MCPClient
```

```
client = MCPClient(
    url="http://localhost:8000/mcp",
    auth_token="secret-token",
    timeout=10
)

def get_weather(city):
    result = client.call_tool("tool.get_weather", {"city": city})
    return result.result if result and result.result else {"error":
"Weather data unavailable"}

def get_user_profile(user_id):
    result = client.call_resource("resource.user_profile", {"user_id":
user_id})
    return result.result if result and result.result else {"error": "No
profile found"}
```

Step 3: Chatbot Handler (`main.py`)

This is the core logic that merges tool outputs and user context into a
dynamic LLM prompt.

```
import openai
from mcp_client import get_weather, get_user_profile

openai.api_key = "your-openai-key"

def generate_chatbot_response(user_id, message):
    user = get_user_profile(user_id)
    weather = get_weather("New York")

    prompt = f"""
You are a smart assistant for a travel app. Here's the user profile:
{user}

Current weather: {weather}

User says: {message}
```

```
Respond helpfully, concisely, and contextually.
"""

    response = openai.ChatCompletion.create(
        model="gpt-4",
        messages=[{"role": "user", "content": prompt}]
    )

    return response['choices'][0]['message']['content']
```

Step 4: Sample Output

Calling the function:

```
reply = generate_chatbot_response(user_id="u123", message="Should I pack
an umbrella?")
print(reply)
```

Might yield:

"Yes, you should. Based on your location and preferences, and the fact that it's expected to rain in New York today, packing an umbrella is a good idea."

Step 5: Testing and Expanding

- Add fallback logic for missing user profiles.
- Log MCP responses for observability.
- Add more tools like `tool.find_hotels`, `resource.flight_prices`, etc.

Wrap-Up

This hands-on project illustrates how to build a real AI chatbot integrated with MCP. By combining tools (function invocations), resources (context injection), and prompt engineering, you create a responsive, intelligent system that mimics real assistant behavior. With this pattern, you're not just using LLMs statically—you're giving them real-time awareness, dynamic memory, and action-taking capability.

Part III – Advanced Integrations and Use Cases

Chapter 6: Integrating MCP with LangChain Agents

6.1 Where MCP Fits in LangChain Pipelines

MCP fits naturally into LangChain pipelines as a powerful mechanism for extending agent capabilities with real-time tools and contextual data. LangChain is built around the concept of chaining language models with tools, memory, and data sources, and MCP serves as a universal adapter that lets agents dynamically invoke tools and retrieve structured resources from any compliant backend. This integration enhances not just functionality but modularity, enabling agents to scale across domains without tight coupling to specific APIs or logic hardcoded into the app.

When building LangChain agents, you typically define tools as Python callables or wrappers around APIs. With MCP, these tools are abstracted into standardized JSON-RPC interfaces hosted on external MCP servers. The LangChain agent interacts with these tools using simple client calls, which makes them reusable and language-model agnostic.

For example, in a customer support agent pipeline, you can use MCP to externalize functions like `tool.lookup_order_status` or `resource.customer_profile`. These are not local methods but remote functions accessed via an MCP client. This decouples your application logic from the AI model itself and introduces a clean, scalable integration point. When you compose LangChain agents, you simply register MCP-based tools using LangChain's `Tool` interface and configure the prompt templates to pass appropriate arguments.

In summary, MCP acts as a connective layer that plugs seamlessly into LangChain's architecture. It enables a clean separation between AI reasoning and external execution, providing agents with the power to perform tasks, access live data, and reason over structured knowledge without hard dependencies. This makes your LangChain workflows both cleaner to manage and more powerful in production scenarios.

6.2 Registering MCP as a Tool and Retriever

Registering MCP as both a Tool and a Retriever in a LangChain agent architecture allows your AI workflows to interact seamlessly with external functions and structured data—using a common, scalable interface. LangChain supports integration with custom tools and retrievers by wrapping callable interfaces or data fetchers into classes that conform to its agent execution model. MCP tools and resources, implemented as JSON-RPC methods on a server, can be treated the same way: as callable tools or document retrievers dynamically queried by the agent at runtime.

To register an MCP Tool in LangChain, you first create a lightweight Python client that connects to your MCP server. This client issues JSON-RPC requests using the standard `method` and `params` format, returning structured responses. For instance, suppose your MCP server exposes a `tool.get_weather(city: str)` function. You can wrap it in a LangChain-compatible `Tool` class by implementing a function that takes in input strings, forwards them via MCP, and formats the result into an agent-readable response. You then instantiate LangChain's `Tool` object by supplying a `name`, a `description`, and your callable function.

```python
from langchain.tools import Tool
import requests
import json

def mcp_weather_tool(city: str) -> str:
    payload = {
        "jsonrpc": "2.0",
        "id": "weather-req",
        "method": "tool.get_weather",
        "params": {"city": city}
    }
    response = requests.post("http://localhost:5001/jsonrpc",
json=payload)
    result = response.json()
    return f"The weather in {city} is
{result['result']['summary']}."

weather_tool = Tool(
    name="WeatherLookup",
    description="Use this tool to get the current weather for
a given city.",
```

```
        func=mcp_weather_tool
)
```

This tool can now be injected into any LangChain agent pipeline as part of its action set. The agent will invoke it as needed based on prompt instructions and model reasoning.

MCP can also serve as a Retriever. Imagine an MCP resource method like `resource.search_documents(query: str)` that returns relevant textual chunks. You can adapt this into LangChain's retriever interface by subclassing `BaseRetriever` and implementing the `get_relevant_documents` method. This lets agents fetch context at runtime from remote sources like databases, CRMs, or knowledge graphs, using a unified protocol.

```
from langchain.schema import Document
from langchain.retrievers import BaseRetriever

class MCPRetriever(BaseRetriever):
    def get_relevant_documents(self, query: str):
        payload = {
            "jsonrpc": "2.0",
            "id": "search-req",
            "method": "resource.search_documents",
            "params": {"query": query}
        }
        response =
requests.post("http://localhost:5001/jsonrpc", json=payload)
        docs = response.json()["result"]["documents"]
        return [Document(page_content=doc["text"],
metadata={"source": doc["source"]}) for doc in docs]
```

Once registered, this retriever can be passed into any LangChain memory module, conversational chain, or RetrievalQA pipeline, ensuring the agent always has relevant, context-rich input without hardcoding any backend access logic.

To conclude, MCP's standardization via JSON-RPC makes it trivial to integrate with LangChain's flexible tool and retriever interfaces. This gives your agents the ability to interact with dynamic data and execute structured operations—all while maintaining clear separation between model reasoning and backend logic.

6.3 LangChain Agent Code Walkthrough with MCP

Integrating an MCP server into a LangChain agent pipeline brings external tools and dynamic data retrieval directly into the reasoning flow of your AI application. In this section, we'll walk through the full implementation of a LangChain agent that uses both an MCP-registered tool and an MCP-backed retriever, illustrating how to wire up context-aware functionality end-to-end using only JSON-RPC interfaces and LangChain's abstraction layers.

Let's begin by assuming you have an MCP server running locally at `http://localhost:5001/jsonrpc`, exposing two endpoints: a `tool.get_weather(city)` function and a `resource.search_documents(query)` method. These will be integrated into a LangChain agent that can both retrieve relevant knowledge and perform a function call when asked a question like "What's the weather in Berlin today?" or "Summarize recent updates about electric vehicles."

First, we define the MCP tool wrapper using a callable Python function. This function takes user input, constructs the JSON-RPC payload, and submits it to the MCP server via HTTP POST.

```python
import requests
from langchain.tools import Tool

def get_weather_from_mcp(city: str) -> str:
    payload = {
        "jsonrpc": "2.0",
        "id": "weather-1",
        "method": "tool.get_weather",
        "params": {"city": city}
    }
    response = requests.post("http://localhost:5001/jsonrpc",
json=payload)
    data = response.json()
    return f"Weather in {city}: {data['result']['summary']}"
```

We then register this as a LangChain `Tool` that the agent will recognize by name and description.

```python
weather_tool = Tool(
```

```
    name="GetWeather",
    description="Provides the current weather for a specified
city.",
    func=get_weather_from_mcp
)
```

Next, we implement an MCP retriever by subclassing `BaseRetriever`. This lets our agent pull in up-to-date external information as context, using natural language queries.

```
from langchain.schema import Document
from langchain.retrievers import BaseRetriever

class MCPContextRetriever(BaseRetriever):
    def get_relevant_documents(self, query: str):
        payload = {
            "jsonrpc": "2.0",
            "id": "context-1",
            "method": "resource.search_documents",
            "params": {"query": query}
        }
        response =
requests.post("http://localhost:5001/jsonrpc", json=payload)
        docs = response.json().get("result",
{}).get("documents", [])
        return [Document(page_content=doc["text"],
metadata=doc.get("metadata", {})) for doc in docs]
```

This retriever can now be plugged into a conversational retrieval chain, like a `RetrievalQA` agent or even a tool-augmented agent depending on your architecture. For this walkthrough, we'll use a basic `initialize_agent` setup using OpenAI functions and our MCP tool:

```
from langchain.agents import initialize_agent, AgentType
from langchain.chat_models import ChatOpenAI

llm = ChatOpenAI(temperature=0.3)

agent = initialize_agent(
    tools=[weather_tool],
    llm=llm,
    agent=AgentType.OPENAI_FUNCTIONS,
    verbose=True
```

```
)
```

Now you can call the agent with natural queries and see how it chooses to use the `GetWeather` tool if the question involves a city and weather context.

```
response = agent.run("What's the weather like in Lagos
today?")
print(response)
```

To incorporate the retriever into a more context-aware pipeline, you would initialize a retrieval-augmented chain like so:

```
from langchain.chains import RetrievalQA

retriever = MCPContextRetriever()
contextual_chain = RetrievalQA.from_chain_type(
    llm=llm,
    retriever=retriever,
    return_source_documents=True
)

output = contextual_chain.run("Summarize the latest updates
on clean energy.")
print(output)
```

This complete setup demonstrates how an MCP server becomes the centralized interface between LangChain and your application logic or knowledge backend. Tools expose structured operations like APIs, while resources serve as indexed knowledge streams or database-backed context. The LangChain agent orchestrates both seamlessly, turning natural language prompts into action using the standard JSON-RPC 2.0 protocol.

By adopting this pattern, your AI agents become not only more capable but also more maintainable—since MCP decouples backend capabilities from frontend orchestration and keeps each layer modular and easily testable.

6.4 Pros and Cons of Using MCP in LangChain

Using the Model Context Protocol (MCP) within a LangChain pipeline introduces powerful extensibility, enabling developers to connect agents with external tools and dynamic contextual data through a standardized, language-agnostic interface. But like any architectural choice, this integration comes with both clear benefits and notable trade-offs that must be understood to build reliable, scalable AI systems.

The primary advantage of using MCP in LangChain is the clean separation of concerns it affords. By decoupling tool execution and context retrieval into MCP endpoints, developers can maintain and evolve these components independently of the agent orchestration layer. For example, an LLM agent defined in LangChain can call a `tool.analyze_financials` method exposed by an MCP server written in Go, Python, or any language that speaks JSON-RPC. This promotes polyglot development and makes backend services easier to test, scale, and monitor separately from the LLM logic.

MCP also brings improved composability. LangChain tools and retrievers backed by MCP endpoints are modular, making it straightforward to add new capabilities, swap implementations, or run tools behind secure interfaces without changing the agent's logic. This is especially valuable in production environments, where robust API surface control and secure context delivery are critical.

Another benefit is runtime flexibility. Since MCP tools and resources are defined dynamically, agents can interact with live systems—like querying up-to-date weather, invoking proprietary analytics functions, or accessing a knowledge graph—without pre-embedding all logic in the LangChain pipeline. This opens the door to real-time, intelligent agents capable of reacting to evolving external state and user needs.

However, there are some trade-offs to account for. The first is latency. Because every MCP call involves an HTTP POST over the network with JSON encoding/decoding, each tool invocation or context retrieval adds measurable delay. In scenarios requiring multiple chained calls (e.g., search → extract → summarize), this can accumulate into noticeable lag. Developers may need to optimize endpoints for low-latency response and consider caching where appropriate.

Second, debugging becomes more involved. Since LangChain agents are often orchestrating calls across an LLM, a JSON-RPC server, and potentially third-party APIs behind the MCP interface, tracing failures or unexpected outputs requires monitoring logs across several services. A well-instrumented MCP server with structured logging, request IDs, and replay tooling becomes essential.

Finally, while MCP adds standardization, it also introduces operational overhead. You need to deploy and maintain a server infrastructure for your MCP tools and resources, handle authentication, secure communication, and version compatibility—all of which may be unnecessary for simpler prototypes or internal-only tools. This makes MCP ideal for teams building serious, long-lived agent systems—but possibly overkill for one-off scripts or toy apps.

In short, MCP elevates LangChain agent architectures into enterprise-ready, modular systems by introducing clean protocol boundaries and reusable interfaces. When building robust, multi-agent applications or AI workflows that must evolve over time, this integration pays off. But for quick hacks or latency-sensitive edge cases, the added complexity may not be justified. Choose the architecture that aligns with your goals—and be ready to evolve as your agent systems grow.

6.5 Use Case: Real-Time Q&A Using LangChain + MCP

Real-time question answering (Q&A) is one of the most compelling use cases for integrating LangChain agents with the Model Context Protocol (MCP). By combining LangChain's orchestration and prompt chaining with MCP's structured access to external tools and live resources, developers can build agents that not only understand complex queries but also dynamically retrieve the freshest, most relevant information at runtime—something that static context windows or pre-loaded embeddings can't offer alone.

To illustrate this, imagine you're building a Q&A agent for a logistics company that helps human operators quickly resolve shipment issues. The agent must answer questions like "Where is shipment #AX98324 currently located?" or "Which shipments are delayed more than 48 hours?" These answers can't come from the LLM's static knowledge—they require real-time data access.

Here's how the solution unfolds step-by-step using LangChain with MCP:

You first implement an MCP server that exposes two components: a `tool.track_shipment` function (which queries a live logistics database by tracking number) and a `resource.delay_report` endpoint (which returns a JSON feed of delayed shipments from a monitoring system). These are registered using JSON-RPC as callable methods. The `tool.track_shipment` accepts a tracking number and returns a structured response like current location, estimated delivery time, and status. The `resource.delay_report` returns a filtered list of delayed shipments, dynamically generated from real-time data.

On the LangChain side, you define a `StructuredTool` that calls the MCP server using the LangChain-compatible JSON-RPC client. The tool's schema includes required input fields (`tracking_number` for instance), a description, and an output parser that formats the result into a readable answer.

Now, when a user types a question into the chatbot UI, LangChain routes the prompt to the LLM. The LLM detects the intent (e.g., track shipment) and generates a structured tool call. LangChain then executes the tool by sending the request to the MCP server. Once the response is received, it's inserted back into the ongoing prompt chain so the LLM can generate a final, human-readable response—like "Shipment AX98324 is currently in Dallas, Texas, and is expected to arrive in Chicago by 3 PM tomorrow."

What makes this setup powerful is the separation of concerns: the LLM doesn't need internal access to the database or understand the API surface—it just needs to know the tool schema and when to use it. The MCP server abstracts and isolates the business logic, enabling secure, maintainable integration.

In production, you can further enhance this system with logging and monitoring via LangChain callbacks or AgentOps plugins, and implement caching on the MCP server to reduce load on expensive real-time queries.

In summary, LangChain + MCP enables real-time, accurate Q&A agents that bridge LLM reasoning with live, trustworthy backend data—without hard-coding business logic into your prompts or agents. This architecture is robust, scalable, and well-suited to enterprise-grade assistant applications across logistics, finance, healthcare, and beyond.

Chapter 7: MCP in Autonomous Agents like AutoGPT

7.1 Understanding AutoGPT and ReAct Architectures

Understanding AutoGPT and ReAct architectures is crucial for developers aiming to build autonomous AI agents that operate without constant human prompts. These architectures define how agents reason, decide, and act in a loop, typically using language models as the brain and surrounding tools, memory, or APIs to interface with the external world. AutoGPT represents one of the earliest and most popular implementations of such an autonomous agent, while ReAct (short for *Reasoning and Acting*) is a framework proposed to structure the agent's decision-making by alternating between internal reasoning steps and external tool invocations.

AutoGPT operates through a loop where the language model is repeatedly prompted to assess its current goals, generate a plan, execute actions via tools (typically APIs), and evaluate the outcomes. The system feeds the LLM a chain-of-thought prompt that includes the current objective, relevant past steps, and available tools. The output includes the next action, rationale, and any necessary parameters. AutoGPT often uses a command registry or plugin interface, where each tool or command is a Python function that maps directly to a defined action type—such as searching Google, reading a file, or updating a memory store.

ReAct builds on this by structuring prompts with explicit "Thought" and "Action" segments. The LLM reasons out loud about the problem (Thought), chooses an appropriate tool or command (Action), and then receives an observation from that action's output. This loop continues until the LLM reaches a final answer or terminates its task. The design encourages more interpretable reasoning and structured decision-making compared to raw freeform generation.

Let's illustrate how this works with a simple real-world example: suppose you're building an AutoGPT-like agent tasked with planning a weekend trip. The objective is: "Book a hotel in Paris for this weekend under $200/night and find nearby attractions." The agent begins with the Thought: *"I need to find available hotels in Paris within the budget range."* It then issues an Action: `search_hotels(location="Paris", max_price=200, dates="this weekend")`. The result (Observation) returns three hotels. The agent evaluates and thinks: *"The second hotel is affordable and well-rated. Next, I'll find attractions nearby."* It proceeds with an Action like `get_nearby_attractions(hotel_id="H234")`, followed by further planning. Each tool call is a discrete, structured action, and the system keeps a memory of all past steps, results, and rationale.

In practice, developers implement this loop by wrapping LLM prompts inside a Python control flow that performs the tool execution, maintains logs of thought/action/observation cycles, and handles fail-safes like timeouts, empty results, or hallucinations. ReAct-based systems, in particular, can be implemented using LangChain or custom orchestration frameworks, ensuring the agent doesn't drift too far from interpretable and bounded logic.

In both AutoGPT and ReAct, the use of structured protocols like MCP dramatically improves the design. By exposing external tools and resources as callable endpoints through a consistent interface, MCP allows these agents to delegate tasks like data lookup, content retrieval, or API calls without hardwiring business logic into the prompt. As a result, the agent remains modular, testable, and adaptable.

In summary, understanding how AutoGPT and ReAct structure agent behavior is foundational for designing effective autonomous systems. These architectures enable continuous, iterative problem-solving, and when paired with MCP, they unlock scalable, secure, and production-grade deployments that can work across domains—from travel planning to enterprise automation.

7.2 Plugging MCP Tools into Autonomous Loops

Integrating MCP tools into autonomous loops such as those used by AutoGPT or ReAct-based agents transforms these agents from isolated reasoning engines into powerful orchestrators capable of real-world interaction. The core idea behind this integration is to expose external functionalities—like searching a database, hitting an API, or running a calculation—as MCP tools, which the agent can invoke during its thought-action-observation cycle. The MCP server acts as a mediator that registers tools and standardizes how they are invoked using JSON-RPC, while the agent's runtime dynamically calls these tools when needed, using structured prompts and handler functions.

To plug MCP tools into an autonomous loop, the process begins by registering your tools on an MCP server. For instance, consider a tool called `weather_lookup` that retrieves current weather data for a city. The MCP tool is defined with metadata including a name, a description, input parameters, and a function endpoint that handles the logic. Once registered, this tool is advertised to the client (the autonomous agent) through the MCP handshake process, where the agent receives a schema describing available tools.

Here's how a real interaction would flow in code. Suppose you're building an AutoGPT-style agent with a task: "Tell me if I should bring an umbrella to Paris today." After processing this task and planning its next step, the agent identifies the need for weather data. It generates the following action in its reasoning loop:

```
{
  "method": "weather_lookup",
  "params": {
    "city": "Paris"
  }
}
```

The MCP client running inside the agent app sends this JSON-RPC request to the MCP server. The server invokes the registered `weather_lookup` function, which fetches the forecast using a third-party weather API and returns a structured response like:

```
{
  "result": {
    "condition": "Rain",
    "temperature": 17,
    "advice": "Yes, bring an umbrella."
  }
}
```

The agent then integrates this response back into its reasoning chain as an observation and continues planning. It may choose to issue a follow-up action or conclude the task depending on the response. This tool invocation happens asynchronously in code, usually wrapped in a loop where the LLM outputs the next intended action, and the orchestrator (e.g., a LangChain agent loop or custom logic) routes the call to the appropriate MCP tool.

Crucially, MCP abstracts away the underlying implementation details of the tools. Whether the `weather_lookup` tool hits a REST API, scrapes a website, or queries a local CSV doesn't matter to the agent. It simply sees a callable interface with clear input/output schema, making reasoning more predictable and repeatable.

Developers can further enhance the experience by auto-generating tool documentation from MCP metadata and embedding that in the agent's system prompt. This allows the LLM to better understand which tools are available and how to use them effectively, minimizing hallucination and maximizing task efficiency.

In summary, plugging MCP tools into autonomous loops allows AI agents to act on the world around them in a structured, scalable, and modular way. It eliminates brittle prompt-only designs and instead brings in a formal, code-based execution layer where external tools are first-class citizens. This integration gives developers the power to build robust autonomous systems that blend reasoning with real-time data and actionable services—critical for deploying production-grade AI workflows.

7.3 External Context Injection for Adaptive Behavior

Injecting external context into autonomous agents using the Model Context Protocol (MCP) is a pivotal step toward making their behavior adaptive, responsive, and relevant to real-world conditions. Unlike static prompts or pre-defined rules, external context allows agents to shift behavior dynamically based on the most current data—whether that's user history, operational state, sensor readings, or real-time business metrics. MCP enables this through its `resource` interface, which allows agents to retrieve structured external data on demand, without hardcoding source logic or embedding stale information in prompts.

The process begins with defining an MCP resource on the server side. A resource behaves like a read-only tool—it doesn't take arbitrary commands or change the environment, but it returns data that is used to influence decision-making. For example, you might define a `customer_profile` resource that, given a `user_id`, returns past purchase behavior, sentiment score, and support history. Here's a resource definition skeleton in code:

```
@resource(name="customer_profile", description="Returns
context for a given user ID")
```

```
def get_customer_profile(user_id: str) -> dict:
    # Simulated lookup from a CRM database
    return {
        "user_id": user_id,
        "purchases": ["Laptop", "Monitor"],
        "sentiment": "Positive",
        "support_tickets": 2
    }
```

Once the resource is available on the MCP server, the client (i.e., the autonomous agent) can query it as part of its reasoning loop. Suppose the task is: *"Suggest an upsell offer for returning customers."* The agent begins by querying the `customer_profile` resource:

```
{
  "method": "customer_profile",
  "params": {
    "user_id": "u7845"
  }
}
```

The MCP server responds with the structured context, and the client parses this into its internal scratchpad or observation memory. From there, the LLM receives a contextualized prompt:

"You are an upsell assistant. The customer has previously purchased: Laptop, Monitor. Sentiment is Positive. There are 2 open support tickets. Based on this, suggest a personalized upsell item and justification."

This pattern dramatically improves agent performance, especially in multi-turn or goal-oriented systems. It reduces hallucinations, boosts grounding in reality, and creates a clean boundary between reasoning and context provisioning. The agent does not need to embed massive context windows or perform RAG; it simply retrieves what it needs through a lightweight, API-style call to a resource.

From a system design perspective, MCP decouples data provisioning from agent logic. You can upgrade how a resource computes its data—e.g., from flat-file lookups to real-time ML models—without touching the agent's reasoning code. It also allows developers to set access controls, cache strategies, or limit rates at the protocol level, maintaining control over external context exposure.

To summarize, external context injection through MCP resources empowers autonomous agents to behave adaptively, making informed decisions based on up-to-the-minute information. This makes agents far more reliable, especially in enterprise, user-centric, or operational environments where dynamic inputs are not optional but critical. MCP makes this integration elegant, scalable, and maintainable, placing contextual intelligence at the heart of next-gen AI agents.

7.4 Scenario Walkthrough: AutoGPT with MCP and External Data

To fully grasp the power of MCP in autonomous systems, consider a scenario where AutoGPT is tasked with monitoring a fleet of retail stores and taking proactive actions based on real-time operational data. This walkthrough demonstrates how MCP can be used to inject external context into AutoGPT's reasoning loop—enabling informed, autonomous decisions. We'll step through the architecture, setup, and runtime behavior, focusing on a real-world scenario that blends adaptive logic with dynamic data provisioning.

Scenario: AutoGPT Monitoring Retail Store Operations

The task for AutoGPT is to monitor sales performance across multiple store branches and initiate restock recommendations or flag anomalies when necessary. The environment includes a set of MCP resources hosted on an MCP server that return live data such as sales metrics, inventory levels, and weather conditions, which can influence foot traffic.

Step 1: Define the MCP Resources

We begin by exposing operational data as MCP resources. Here are three sample resource functions hosted on the MCP server:

```
@resource(name="sales_data", description="Returns hourly sales for a
store location")
def get_sales_data(store_id: str) -> dict:
    return {
        "store_id": store_id,
        "sales": 1250,
        "timestamp": "2025-06-09T12:00:00Z"
```

```
    }

@resource(name="inventory_levels", description="Returns inventory status
for a store")
def get_inventory(store_id: str) -> dict:
    return {
        "store_id": store_id,
        "low_stock_items": ["milk", "detergent"]
    }

@resource(name="local_weather", description="Returns the current weather
condition for a store location")
def get_weather(store_id: str) -> dict:
    return {
        "store_id": store_id,
        "weather": "Rainy"
    }
```

Each resource is lightweight, returns structured JSON data, and can be accessed via simple JSON-RPC calls.

Step 2: Plug Resources into AutoGPT's Reasoning Loop

AutoGPT operates with a goal-driven loop: plan, execute, and verify. We modify its planning step to call MCP resources before deciding on next actions. A sample prompt passed to the LLM might look like this:

"Store ID: 202
Current Sales: 1250
Weather: Rainy
Low Stock Items: milk, detergent

Based on this data, determine if the store requires a restock order, a promotional offer to improve sales, or both. Justify your recommendation."

AutoGPT fetches this context using its internal tools registered against the MCP resource endpoints. This happens either through wrapper classes or via direct MCP client calls in the execution logic.

Step 3: Reason, Act, and Observe

With the context retrieved, the agent generates a proposed plan such as:

"Due to low foot traffic (Rainy weather) and moderate sales, initiate a local promotional SMS campaign for umbrellas. Also, trigger a restock alert for milk and detergent."

AutoGPT then dispatches follow-up actions via its toolset—such as sending API calls to the store's campaign manager system or notifying warehouse systems for restocking. This shows how context flows directly from MCP into decisions and actions.

Step 4: Feedback Loop and Adaptation

Suppose the sales remain flat despite promotions. In the next loop iteration, AutoGPT checks sales again and updates its strategy—perhaps escalating to regional managers or suggesting a temporary closure. This adaptability is powered by dynamic, real-time context made available through MCP.

Wrap-Up

This walkthrough illustrates how AutoGPT, when integrated with the Model Context Protocol, transforms from a generic text agent into a domain-aware, data-driven decision-maker. By cleanly decoupling logic from data sources, MCP allows agents to interact with real-world systems while staying stateless, modular, and maintainable. The result is an architecture where intelligence emerges not just from large models—but from timely, contextual information flowing through a well-structured protocol.

7.5 Do's and Don'ts When Using MCP with Self-Driven Agents

When integrating the Model Context Protocol (MCP) with self-driven agents like AutoGPT, developers must balance flexibility with discipline. While MCP enables powerful real-time context injection and function invocation, careless implementation can lead to confusion, inefficiency, or even unintended behavior. This section provides a practical, experience-driven guide to what works well—and what to avoid—when building autonomous agents that rely on MCP.

First, always design your MCP resources and tools to be deterministic and lightweight. Self-driven agents loop frequently, often querying context multiple times per minute. If your MCP server exposes slow or stateful resources, the agent's performance can degrade rapidly. Keep your tools stateless, idempotent, and bounded in execution time. For instance, a tool that returns the current inventory level for a store should not perform deep analytical computations or depend on mutable session state—just retrieve data and return it.

Second, enforce strict input validation and output formatting on all MCP interfaces. One common mistake is to assume the LLM will always produce clean, well-structured inputs when invoking tools. In practice, language models can hallucinate field names, miss required parameters, or introduce malformed JSON. Always wrap your tools with a validation layer, and reject requests that don't conform to expected formats with clear error messages. Likewise, tools should return simple, well-defined outputs. Avoid deeply nested or ambiguous structures, as LLMs can struggle to parse or use them effectively in subsequent steps.

Third, minimize cross-dependencies between tools and resources. An agent's autonomy thrives on modularity. If your tools require complex chaining logic or rely on each other's intermediate outputs, you risk turning your orchestration layer into a brittle, tightly coupled system. It's better to delegate planning and reasoning back to the LLM agent, allowing it to call tools individually with fresh prompts informed by prior results, rather than designing tools to orchestrate each other internally.

On the other hand, one of the most effective MCP practices in autonomous loops is context layering—starting with a minimal context (e.g., user goal or recent conversation), then dynamically injecting data from MCP resources as the agent explores solutions. This technique improves grounding, encourages clarity, and avoids overwhelming the model with irrelevant context. For example, only call the `inventory_levels` resource if the task involves procurement or logistics. Don't preload every possible context upfront.

Also avoid the anti-pattern of overloading the agent with decision authority. Just because the LLM *can* access all context doesn't mean it *should*. Incorporate structured control flows where needed. For instance, use system-level policies (e.g., max budget per order or blackout times for sending emails) to constrain what actions the agent can take, even if the LLM proposes otherwise. This guards against unintended or unsafe outcomes.

In summary, use MCP as a precision instrument—not a blunt pipe to dump all possible data into the agent. Build clean, reusable tools; enforce strict input/output contracts; allow the agent to drive sequencing; and always sandbox its authority with clear boundaries. When done right, MCP transforms self-driven agents into reliable collaborators, capable of navigating complex workflows with situational awareness and discipline. When done carelessly, it leads to confusion, error cascades, or untrustworthy behavior.

Chapter 8: Monitoring, Metrics, and AgentOps

8.1 The AgentOps Mindset: Observability for AI

As AI agents transition from experiments to production-ready systems, observability becomes mission-critical. AgentOps—a blend of operations and agent intelligence—emphasizes that maintaining visibility, traceability, and control over AI agents is not optional; it's foundational. Just like DevOps revolutionized software reliability through continuous integration and monitoring, AgentOps does the same for AI agents by enabling transparent, auditable, and measurable execution at every level.

Observability in the context of Model Context Protocol (MCP)-enabled agents begins with logging. Every invocation of a tool or resource through MCP should produce structured logs, capturing key metadata: method name, input parameters, timestamps, latency, and outputs. For example, when an MCP agent calls a `get_user_preferences` tool, the system should log the session ID, tool name, inputs (e.g., user ID), and output summary. These logs form the basis for debugging and retrospective analysis.

Beyond logging, metrics are essential for operational health. Track metrics such as tool usage frequency, average response time, failure rates, and context size over time. This can reveal patterns like degraded performance when agents use certain tools or excessive context leading to token bloat. Visualization dashboards—built using open platforms like Prometheus and Grafana or services like Datadog—can help teams detect anomalies, bottlenecks, and regressions in real time.

Equally important is traceability. AI agents don't always behave predictably. You need lineage: a trace of each decision, context used, and MCP interaction that led to the final outcome. This is especially true in regulated industries where compliance and audit trails are mandatory. AgentOps tooling should support distributed tracing across multiple tool/resource calls within a session, giving developers and reviewers a step-by-step timeline of agent behavior.

Another AgentOps principle is observability-driven development. Rather than adding logs reactively, design tools and prompts to emit relevant signals from day one. For instance, enrich output payloads with diagnostic metadata, such as confidence scores or execution paths. Combine this with telemetry hooks in the agent orchestration logic to surface "why" a decision was made—not just "what" was done.

Finally, observability also feeds feedback loops. By capturing logs and metrics, teams can identify underperforming prompts, stale resource endpoints, or misused tools. This allows for continuous improvement cycles: refining prompts, optimizing tool logic, and retraining LLM wrappers as needed.

In short, the AgentOps mindset treats every agent like a production service—one that must be observable, debuggable, and measurable. By applying the same rigor we bring to traditional backend services—structured logging, metrics, tracing, and proactive monitoring—we ensure that autonomous agents don't become opaque or untrustworthy. Instead, we create AI systems that are not only intelligent but also accountable, traceable, and operable at scale.

8.2 Tracking Calls, Tools Used, and Latency with MCP

Tracking interactions across MCP-enabled AI agents is a cornerstone of observability and performance diagnostics. Every time an agent initiates a request—whether it's calling a tool, retrieving context via a resource, or completing a task—it generates critical metadata that should be captured: the method invoked, time taken, parameters passed, and the success or failure of the operation. This data isn't just for logging purposes; it becomes the backbone for operational insight, optimization, and accountability within AgentOps workflows.

Using the MCP JSON-RPC format, every interaction begins with a structured `request` object that includes a unique `id`, a `method` name such as `"tool.weather_lookup"`, and a `params` object containing the arguments. The MCP server responds with a corresponding `response` that includes a `result` or an `error`, along with the same `id` for correlation. By instrumenting your MCP server to log both the incoming request and the outgoing response, you can create a complete transaction log for every tool invocation. These logs should include timestamps at the entry and exit points of the handler function, allowing you to compute precise latency metrics.

Let's walk through a concrete example. Suppose your AI agent issues a call to a tool named `get_weather_forecast` via MCP. The request body might look like this:

```json
{
  "jsonrpc": "2.0",
  "id": "req-2049",
  "method": "tool.get_weather_forecast",
  "params": {
    "city": "Sydney",
    "unit": "celsius"
  }
}
```

As soon as the server receives this request, you log the timestamp and method name. After the function completes, say in 220 milliseconds, you record the completion timestamp and calculate the round-trip latency. The server's response might be:

```json
{
  "jsonrpc": "2.0",
  "id": "req-2049",
  "result": {
    "forecast": "Partly cloudy, 21°C"
  }
}
```

Now, your log entry includes: the method `"tool.get_weather_forecast"`, the request duration `220ms`, input parameters, output size, and status (`success`). You can store this in a structured log format like JSON Lines or ship it to a centralized observability backend such as ELK Stack, Loki, or CloudWatch Logs.

To go deeper, track the frequency of each tool and resource used. Over time, you'll discover patterns—for instance, that `get_weather_forecast` is called 10x more frequently during early mornings, or that `summarize_article` has the highest error rate due to malformed inputs. These insights enable proactive tuning, like refining input validation or caching popular endpoints.

Additionally, tracking latency helps identify bottlenecks. If a specific resource consistently takes over 1,000ms, it could indicate inefficient data fetching or serialization. This allows teams to isolate and improve slow components before they degrade user experience.

In short, tracking MCP calls, tool usage, and latency isn't just a technical nicety—it's the heartbeat of maintaining performant and trustworthy AI systems. Instrument your infrastructure to collect and analyze this data in real time, and your agents will reward you with improved reliability, transparency, and responsiveness.

8.3 Cost and Performance Metrics for Prompt Chains

Tracking cost and performance metrics for prompt chains is essential for operating MCP-powered AI systems at scale. As agents invoke multiple LLM calls and tools across a single task flow, developers must gain clear visibility into how much each interaction costs in terms of tokens, compute time, and latency—especially when those calls cascade across multiple prompts and services. Without this observability, teams risk runaway costs, hidden inefficiencies, and a lack of actionable insight into how their AI workflows behave in real-world conditions.

In a typical MCP prompt chain, the agent may start by invoking a resource for background context, then pass that context into a summarization tool, which in turn feeds a final decision prompt. Each of these steps involves input and output tokens, function execution, and potentially multiple API calls. To track costs accurately, instrument your MCP server and client layers to record three main metrics: token usage per call (input/output), execution latency, and total chain cost.

Let's walk through a realistic example. Assume your prompt chain performs the following sequence:

1. Call to `resource.retrieve_research_data` (external context).
2. Output piped into `tool.summarize_research`.
3. Summary passed to `tool.generate_recommendation`.

Each step involves calling an LLM endpoint with a distinct prompt. Your MCP client should log the token count for each request and response by inspecting the LLM's return metadata, typically provided in OpenAI-style responses under fields like `usage.prompt_tokens` and `usage.completion_tokens`. Similarly, you should log the latency of each call and the total cumulative runtime.

Here's a simplified snippet of a structured log after executing a full prompt chain:

```json
{
  "chain_id": "chain-8791",
  "steps": [
    {
      "tool": "resource.retrieve_research_data",
      "input_tokens": 120,
      "output_tokens": 850,
      "latency_ms": 310,
      "cost_usd": 0.0015
    },
    {
      "tool": "tool.summarize_research",
      "input_tokens": 850,
      "output_tokens": 300,
      "latency_ms": 540,
      "cost_usd": 0.0021
    },
    {
      "tool": "tool.generate_recommendation",
      "input_tokens": 300,
      "output_tokens": 100,
      "latency_ms": 260,
      "cost_usd": 0.0009
    }
  ],
  "total_tokens": 1720,
  "total_latency_ms": 1110,
  "total_cost_usd": 0.0045
}
```

By aggregating this data across sessions and users, you can calculate average cost per task, detect inefficient chains, and even implement automated guardrails—such as aborting chains that exceed a predefined budget or time threshold. You might find that a summarization tool accounts for 70% of your monthly token spend, prompting an optimization effort using a smaller model or a prompt template redesign.

Furthermore, you can correlate performance with business KPIs. For example, how much does a successful customer support resolution cost in token and compute terms? What is the latency-to-satisfaction ratio in your user feedback loop? These are operational insights that turn raw observability data into strategic decision-making.

In summary, prompt chains in MCP-powered agents are not black boxes. They are measurable, analyzable sequences of interaction, and capturing their cost and performance metrics is a foundational step toward creating scalable, efficient, and production-grade AI systems. Build your observability stack early, and ensure that every token and every millisecond is accounted for.

8.4 Debugging Agent Failures in Production

Debugging agent failures in production within an MCP-enabled environment requires a disciplined, systematic approach—one that combines structured logging, contextual metadata, and fast access to request histories. Because MCP agents interact across modular tools, resources, and prompts, errors can arise at multiple layers: malformed requests, unreachable endpoints, schema mismatches, authentication failures, or invalid LLM responses. Without the right diagnostic setup, these issues can be opaque and hard to isolate. Your goal as a developer is to make every failure actionable through rich observability and traceable context.

The first step is to ensure your MCP server and clients log all incoming and outgoing JSON-RPC messages in a structured format. This includes full method names, parameters, timestamps, and response payloads. Crucially, each call must be tagged with a unique `session_id` or `trace_id` so that individual workflows can be reconstructed step-by-step. When a tool or resource fails mid-chain, this ID lets you pinpoint exactly where and why the failure occurred.

Let's look at a real-world example. Assume a user triggers a multi-step planning agent that breaks during execution. The trace log might show:

```json
{
  "trace_id": "run-5463",
  "timestamp": "2025-06-09T14:32:10Z",
  "method": "tool.plan_meeting",
  "params": {
    "attendees": ["alice@example.com", "bob@example.com"],
    "timeslot": "2025-06-10T15:00Z"
  },
  "error": {
```

```
  "code": -32602,
  "message": "Invalid timeslot format"
  }
}
```

This immediately tells you the error originated from input formatting—perhaps the calling prompt or LLM tool chain generated the time as a string that didn't match the expected schema. In this case, your fix might involve adding a stricter validation layer on the MCP client side or introducing a pre-processing function that sanitizes inputs before forwarding them to the tool.

In another case, the error might stem from the downstream LLM returning malformed JSON that breaks the tool execution:

```
{
  "trace_id": "run-6748",
  "method": "tool.extract_keywords",
  "response": "Top keywords: innovation, scale, reliability"
}
```

Here, the tool expects a list of keywords as a JSON array, but instead receives a raw string. This is a classic mismatch between model output and function schema. Your debugging strategy might involve reinforcing the output parser or modifying the prompt to force well-structured output. You could even enable schema validation to reject and retry with fallback strategies.

To handle these issues proactively, implement a middleware layer in your MCP stack that wraps every tool/resource invocation in a `try/except` structure and captures the following:

- Method name and inputs
- Exception stack trace
- LLM completion output (if any)
- Caller identity and session ID
- Retry count or backoff status

All of this should be emitted to a centralized logging system like AWS CloudWatch, Azure Monitor, or a custom ELK stack. Consider integrating alerts for repeated failure patterns—e.g., more than five `tool.schedule_task` failures in 10 minutes may signal a broken integration with a calendar API or an expired auth token.

Finally, include a debug mode in your agents that allows verbose inspection of internal decision steps. When enabled, this mode can return a debug payload containing the full chain of reasoning, raw tool outputs, retry attempts, and selected prompts. This is invaluable for fast triage during live issues without needing to replicate the entire environment locally.

In production-grade MCP systems, debugging isn't an afterthought—it's a first-class design feature. By establishing traceable identifiers, enforcing structured logging, and proactively handling known failure modes, you can reduce downtime, accelerate root cause analysis, and build trust in your AI infrastructure.

8.5 Closing the Loop: Learning from Logs and Improving Behavior

Closing the loop in MCP-enabled AI agent systems means turning raw operational logs into actionable feedback that improves agent performance over time. Rather than treating logs as passive records for postmortem analysis, developers should design their systems so that logging actively informs adaptation, refinement, and continual learning. This is especially critical for AI agents that must interact with unpredictable real-world inputs, evolving APIs, and dynamic user intent.

The foundation of this process lies in structured, rich logging across every MCP interaction. Each log entry should capture not only the technical parameters—method names, execution time, tool usage—but also semantic data: what the user asked, what the agent attempted, and what outcome occurred. By aggregating this data across sessions, you can start to observe recurring inefficiencies, ambiguous prompt completions, or error-prone tools.

For example, suppose repeated logs show that a tool called `tool.get_stock_forecast` is frequently invoked with ticker symbols that the tool fails to recognize. By quantifying this failure pattern and surfacing it in dashboards, you can redesign the prompt that generates the stock symbol, add input validation, or integrate an autocomplete resource that filters valid tickers before invocation. This is a direct example of learning from logs to harden the system.

You can also use logs to rank prompts and responses based on effectiveness. If one formulation of a question results in higher tool success rates or lower latency, that prompt variant should become the default. This can be implemented through offline analysis scripts or an active prompt-tuning engine that selects the best-performing version based on historical context and metadata.

Additionally, logs enable you to model confidence heuristics. If certain resources or tools repeatedly yield incomplete or vague results, the agent can learn to trigger a "human-in-the-loop" override or request clarification from the user. Over time, this builds more robust, user-sensitive behavior directly from empirical evidence.

Consider also logging LLM token usage, latency, and cost per request. When combined with success/failure outcomes, this data can drive optimization decisions—such as reducing context size, splitting queries into stages, or replacing expensive tools with cached responses when appropriate.

In practice, closing the loop requires a feedback pipeline: logs are exported to a data store (e.g., BigQuery, Athena, or a NoSQL database), analyzed for patterns via scripts or BI tools, and then those insights are fed back into the prompt library, fallback logic, or resource registry. You might even expose a developer dashboard that surfaces the most common failure modes, slowest tools, or unused capabilities, providing a roadmap for ongoing agent refinement.

Ultimately, MCP systems that evolve based on real-world usage logs become smarter, faster, and more trustworthy. Instead of brittle pipelines that degrade over time, you build living agents that learn from every interaction—closing the loop between operation and improvement.

Part IV – Deploying MCP Systems at Scale

Chapter 9: Real-World Case Studies of MCP in Production

9.1 Enterprise Knowledge Agent in Finance

In the fast-moving world of finance, where data accuracy and timeliness are paramount, deploying MCP-powered agents brings a transformative edge. This section explores a real-world deployment of an Enterprise Knowledge Agent built for a multinational investment firm. The primary objective was to enable internal analysts to query vast volumes of market data, compliance documents, and analyst reports through a natural language interface, while ensuring security, traceability, and low-latency performance.

The architecture centered around a custom MCP server that exposed multiple tools—such as `get_market_snapshot`, `summarize_compliance_report`, and `compare_quarterly_performance`. These tools were implemented using Python microservices backed by secure, read-only APIs into internal databases, Bloomberg terminals, and document management systems. The MCP server was containerized and deployed on AWS Fargate behind a VPC, ensuring isolation, encryption at rest and in transit, and access control via IAM roles and JWT-based authentication.

On the client side, a LangChain-based UI allowed analysts to ask questions like, *"How did our fixed-income portfolio perform compared to Q1 2022?"* or *"Summarize regulatory changes in cross-border trading this year."* The MCP client packaged these queries, automatically selected the relevant tools, and sent structured invocations to the MCP server. Using a context cache and prompt templates optimized for financial terminology, the system delivered accurate answers in under three seconds for 90% of requests.

Monitoring and observability were handled via OpenTelemetry, which logged tool invocation metrics, success rates, and latency per resource. Logs revealed that certain tools failed when compliance documents were unstructured or missing metadata. To address this, the team introduced a pre-processing pipeline that tagged and indexed documents before they were ingested by the summarization resource—an improvement driven directly by production insights.

Importantly, the system supported auditability. Every agent response was linked to its originating data, tool usage, and execution logs. This was crucial for meeting internal compliance standards and external audit requirements. The development team also implemented a lightweight feedback loop, where analysts could rate responses and flag inconsistencies, creating a backlog for continuous improvement.

In short, this financial deployment of MCP demonstrated the protocol's power to unify heterogeneous data systems, expose critical insights safely, and streamline high-value workflows. It validated MCP's suitability for regulated, data-intensive environments where precision, traceability, and adaptability are non-negotiable.

9.2 Developer IDE Assistant with Local Tools via MCP

In modern software development, productivity often hinges on the availability of intelligent, context-aware tools directly within the development environment. This section illustrates how MCP can be used to build a local developer assistant integrated into an IDE—such as VS Code or JetBrains—capable of performing complex AI-assisted tasks using MCP-exposed tools running locally. The assistant enhances developer efficiency by providing real-time, context-aware code suggestions, documentation lookups, and error explanations through a secure, extensible interface.

The architecture involves a lightweight MCP server that runs on the developer's machine and exposes a suite of tools tailored to the local environment. These tools include `explain_error`, `find_usage`, `suggest_refactor`, and `get_docstring`, all of which interact with the local filesystem, language servers, and LLM backends. The server is implemented in Python using FastAPI, and each tool is structured as a callable endpoint that adheres to the MCP JSON-RPC 2.0 specification.

A typical use case begins when a developer encounters a confusing stack trace. Within the IDE, the user highlights the error and invokes the MCP-powered assistant. The MCP client, embedded as an IDE plugin, constructs a JSON-RPC call to the `explain_error` tool, passing the stack trace, project context, and filename. The local server parses the input, checks the codebase for related files or dependencies, and queries an LLM—running either locally or via an API—to generate an explanation and suggested fix. The response is returned to the IDE interface in seconds, with clickable references to the related code lines.

Another example is real-time documentation lookup. When hovering over a function call, the assistant uses the `get_docstring` tool to fetch relevant docstrings or generate one on-the-fly if missing. The assistant can also summarize imported third-party functions by reading the library source or hitting an indexed offline cache. Developers can toggle between the raw documentation and AI-generated summaries without leaving the IDE.

All tool calls are logged locally, with optional anonymized telemetry. To preserve privacy and maintain offline usability, sensitive files and code snippets are never transmitted externally unless explicitly authorized. The developer can configure which tools are enabled and define trust boundaries, ensuring that only whitelisted folders and APIs are accessed during invocation.

By using MCP as the protocol backbone, this local IDE assistant remains modular, extensible, and highly secure. Developers can plug in new tools, adapt them to their coding language, or even override default behaviors with project-specific implementations. The assistant becomes not just a productivity boost, but a context-rich collaborator deeply embedded into the daily development cycle—without ever leaving the local environment.

9.3 IT Automation Using Multiple MCP Tools

In enterprise environments, IT automation is essential for managing infrastructure, responding to incidents, and maintaining system integrity. MCP (Model Context Protocol) introduces a flexible and composable way to build AI-driven automation workflows by exposing reusable tools that can interoperate through structured context. This section demonstrates how MCP can orchestrate multiple tools—each designed for specific IT tasks—into a cohesive automation layer capable of handling tasks such as diagnostics, remediation, and reporting.

Imagine a scenario where a system administrator needs to automate the response to high CPU usage on production servers. Traditionally, this would involve writing complex scripts, setting up cron jobs, and relying on monitoring alerts. With MCP, you can construct a more intelligent, reactive system. The setup involves deploying an MCP server with several purpose-built tools, such as `check_cpu_load`, `restart_service`, `notify_team`, and `log_incident`.

Each of these tools is implemented as a callable JSON-RPC endpoint, designed to operate independently or in combination with others. For instance, `check_cpu_load` collects real-time metrics via SSH or cloud APIs and returns structured data. If the threshold exceeds a defined limit, the orchestration logic (handled by the client or an MCP-aware agent) invokes `restart_service` with the appropriate parameters for the failing process. Simultaneously, `notify_team` triggers an alert through Slack or Microsoft Teams, and `log_incident` writes a record into a centralized log system or a ticketing platform like Jira.

Here's a hands-on walkthrough of this workflow:

1. A watchdog script, running as an MCP client, pings the MCP server every 5 minutes.
2. It sends a request to `check_cpu_load` with the server ID and authentication headers.
3. If the response exceeds 90% CPU utilization, it chains a call to `restart_service`, specifying the process name.
4. Immediately after, it sends a message to `notify_team`, embedding the log and remediation step.
5. Finally, it calls `log_incident` to record the event with timestamps, resolution steps, and the responsible agent.

Each tool returns structured JSON, making it easy to track execution status, fallback to alternative strategies, or raise manual intervention prompts if needed. You can also define conditionals and escalation paths in the orchestration logic to handle more complex cases, such as rebooting the server or scaling out infrastructure via cloud APIs.

Crucially, because MCP abstracts each tool as a well-defined interface, these tools can be reused across other workflows—like patch management, user provisioning, or compliance audits—without rewriting logic. The approach makes your IT automation system modular, context-aware, and easily maintainable. Moreover, logging, error tracing, and auditability are built into each step of the interaction, ensuring that the automation remains secure and transparent for enterprise governance.

By chaining multiple MCP tools in this way, organizations gain a practical, low-friction path to implementing robust AI-augmented automation systems that go beyond basic scripting to deliver intelligent, autonomous operations.

9.4 Lessons from Block, Replit, and Other Early Adopters

Companies like Block, Replit, and other early adopters of agentic infrastructure have provided invaluable real-world insights into the power and challenges of implementing MCP-powered AI systems at scale. Their experiences reveal not just the technical feasibility but the strategic value of adopting the Model Context Protocol to modularize capabilities, isolate responsibilities, and streamline agent-to-agent collaboration in production settings.

At Block, for instance, internal developer tools were enhanced with AI agents that leveraged MCP to interact with secure systems. Instead of a monolithic AI assistant, Block used an MCP server hosting discrete tools for actions like querying internal documentation, checking CI/CD pipeline health, and triggering test deployments. The key lesson was that separating tools into focused JSON-RPC endpoints, all exposed through a common MCP interface, led to better observability, more consistent behavior, and faster debugging. Developers could mix and match tools without refactoring their main agent logic.

Replit's journey was similar but focused more on integrating MCP with a live coding environment. Here, an agent had to manage real-time user input, code execution, and output display—all while being stateless and recoverable. MCP's context passing and resource invocation mechanisms proved critical. By offloading code linting, snippet retrieval, and docstring generation to separate MCP tools, Replit kept the core agent lightweight and reactive. The big win for them was the ability to swap out or upgrade individual tools without breaking the rest of the system—supporting continuous improvement and extensibility.

Another important insight from these companies was around error handling and feedback loops. Both emphasized building structured logging into every tool interaction, which MCP naturally supports via request/response payloads. This allowed them to trace failures, measure tool latency, and adapt prompts or fallback logic in response to drift. Replit even used this data to create dashboards showing tool usage trends and success rates—something that became foundational for their internal AgentOps practices.

Finally, these early adopters stressed the organizational learning that came from modularizing capability. Teams began thinking in terms of reusable tools and clearly defined boundaries. This modular thinking didn't just improve reliability—it accelerated onboarding, reuse, and experimentation. Instead of retraining models or deploying new agents, they added a new MCP tool or tweaked context strategies, often within hours.

In short, early adopters of MCP highlight a repeatable path: start with modular tools, layer in observability and error handling, then evolve through reuse and measurement. Their stories demonstrate that MCP is more than just a protocol—it's an architectural philosophy that enables teams to build intelligent, resilient systems with composable and maintainable parts.

Chapter 10: Best Practices for Production-Grade MCP Systems

10.1 Security and Privacy Standards

As MCP-enabled systems increasingly handle sensitive context, personal data, and high-value logic execution, security and privacy become non-negotiable pillars of a reliable architecture. This section walks through how to apply industry-grade security practices to your MCP server, tools, and client integrations while maintaining developer efficiency and system transparency.

At its foundation, every MCP transaction—whether it's a tool invocation or a resource fetch—flows over JSON-RPC, typically via HTTP. While the protocol itself is agnostic of transport-level encryption, production deployments must enforce HTTPS to prevent eavesdropping and man-in-the-middle attacks. Developers should ensure TLS is properly configured with up-to-date certificates and reject insecure ciphers. If you're deploying on platforms like AWS or Azure, services such as Application Load Balancer or Azure Front Door can offload TLS with built-in WAF (Web Application Firewall) protection.

Authentication and authorization are next. The MCP specification allows for bearer token injection at the transport layer. This gives developers the flexibility to plug in OAuth2, API keys, or JWTs depending on organizational policy. When serving tools that interface with business logic (e.g., payment APIs, HR systems), it's critical to validate that the caller—typically an LLM client—is authorized for that specific function. A clean pattern is to include `client_id` in the token payload and use middleware to reject or allow calls based on scoped permissions.

On the data privacy front, context must be sanitized before serialization. For instance, if a resource retrieves user-specific documents or logs, the server must redact or encrypt sensitive fields before sending them to the LLM. You should never expose raw personally identifiable information (PII) to LLMs unless explicitly required—and even then, log obfuscation and retention policies must comply with data protection laws such as GDPR or HIPAA.

A practical example: let's say you've built an MCP resource that exposes CRM records to the LLM. The server fetches the data from a secure database, strips out customer email addresses and payment information, and logs only anonymized metrics like query latency and volume. Every request is authenticated using a short-lived JWT, and access control is enforced with a role-based system. This gives the LLM useful context without violating privacy principles or compliance standards.

Finally, always include audit logging. MCP requests and responses should be logged with timestamps, client identifiers, method names, and status codes. These logs are essential for forensics, debugging, and demonstrating regulatory compliance. Consider forwarding them to observability stacks like ELK or Datadog, and ensure access to logs is tightly controlled.

In summary, securing MCP-based systems is a multi-layered task involving transport encryption, robust auth policies, sanitized data exposure, and immutable logging. When done right, these practices shield your agents and their users from security breaches and privacy risks—while maintaining the openness and interoperability that make MCP so powerful.

10.2 Fault Tolerance and Retry Strategies

In any production-grade MCP system, failure is not a matter of *if*—it's *when*. Agents operate in environments with transient network glitches, unpredictable latency, API downtime, and incomplete responses from external services or models. A robust MCP-powered AI agent must be built to recover gracefully, retry intelligently, and prevent cascading failures that could compromise user experience or system reliability. Fault tolerance and retry strategies form the foundation for resilience in modern agentic architectures.

At the heart of fault tolerance is controlled retry logic. When an MCP client sends a JSON-RPC call to a remote server—such as invoking a tool or fetching data from a resource—and the response fails or times out, the client must not crash or block indefinitely. Instead, it should retry the call using an **exponential backoff strategy**. For instance, the first retry can be after 500 milliseconds, then 1 second, then 2 seconds. This strategy reduces the risk of overwhelming a failing service and allows transient issues to resolve naturally. If retries are exhausted, a fallback response or error message should be returned to the LLM agent, allowing it to adjust its reasoning path accordingly.

To illustrate, consider a Python-based MCP client making a call to a remote weather.get_forecast tool. Using the tenacity library, you can wrap the call with retry logic like this:

```
from tenacity import retry, stop_after_attempt,
wait_exponential
import mcp

@retry(stop=stop_after_attempt(3),
wait=wait_exponential(multiplier=0.5, min=0.5, max=2))
def get_forecast():
    response = mcp.call_tool("weather.get_forecast",
{"location": "New York"})
    if response["status"] != "ok":
        raise Exception("Weather tool failed")
    return response
```

Timeouts are equally crucial. Without them, a call to a hanging service might freeze the entire agent chain. Both client and server sides should define strict timeouts for every operation. In FastAPI or similar async Python servers, this can be enforced using timeout decorators or async cancellation tokens. Ideally, tools should return an error object if an operation takes longer than a defined threshold (e.g., 3 seconds).

Another effective pattern is **circuit breaking**. If a specific resource or tool fails repeatedly within a short window (e.g., 5 failures in 1 minute), the circuit breaker will stop all traffic to that component temporarily. This prevents retry storms and allows recovery without crashing the system. Libraries like pybreaker support this directly and integrate easily into MCP server-side code.

Fallbacks also play a critical role in fault-tolerant design. Suppose a stock price fetcher tool fails repeatedly. Instead of abandoning the agent's task, the fallback might return cached data or a message like "Real-time data unavailable, using last known value." This gives the agent enough context to proceed and maintain a coherent dialogue.

Finally, ensure **idempotency** in all critical tool operations. For example, if a tool sends an email or writes to a database, retries must not lead to duplicates. Include a unique request_id with each invocation and enforce deduplication on the server side.

In summary, fault tolerance in MCP systems requires deliberate engineering. Implement intelligent retries, strict timeouts, circuit breakers, fallbacks, and idempotent behavior to ensure your agents stay resilient and adaptive—even when the world around them is unreliable. These strategies are not just safety nets—they are essential for delivering intelligent, dependable agent behavior at scale.

10.3 Performance Tuning and Latency Optimization

Performance is one of the most critical success factors for MCP-enabled systems, especially when agents are operating in real-time, latency-sensitive environments. Whether you're orchestrating multi-agent workflows or exposing external resources to LLMs, every millisecond counts. A sluggish response doesn't just slow things down—it breaks the illusion of intelligence. This section walks through practical, hands-on strategies to optimize performance and minimize latency across your MCP architecture.

The first layer of optimization begins at the network level. Since MCP communication is JSON-RPC over HTTP, excessive serialization/deserialization and payload size can introduce lag. Always reduce the payload to just what's necessary—strip verbose logs, compress large context objects, and avoid nesting unless required. For example, a `tool_call` payload that includes an entire document dump in the input parameters should instead pass a content hash or reference ID if the data is already stored and retrievable on the server side.

Caching is a high-leverage tactic. You can cache frequent tool outputs—especially those that depend on static inputs or change infrequently. On the client side, use in-memory stores like `functools.lru_cache` or Redis for external resources such as embeddings, summaries, or configuration templates. On the server side, memoize function outputs that are computationally expensive or call third-party APIs.

Here's a quick server-side example using `functools.lru_cache` in a FastAPI-based MCP tool implementation:

```python
from functools import lru_cache
from fastapi import APIRouter

router = APIRouter()
```

```python
@lru_cache(maxsize=128)
def get_conversion_rate(currency: str):
    # Simulated external API call
    return {"USD": 1.0, "EUR": 0.92}.get(currency, 1.0)


@router.post("/tools/convert_currency")
async def convert_currency(payload: dict):
    rate = get_conversion_rate(payload["currency"])
    return {"amount": payload["amount"] * rate}
```

Next, reduce cold-start latency. If you deploy tools or agents as serverless functions (e.g., Cloud Functions or AWS Lambda), you'll face initialization lag. To avoid this, use containerized deployment on warm infrastructure—like Azure App Services, Google Cloud Run with min instances, or a persistent FastAPI server on a small VM. Also, preload LLMs, retrievers, or vector indexes at startup rather than on demand.

Latency also compounds in chain-of-agent designs. In these workflows, each agent step introduces additional RPC calls and context lookups. You can batch these calls where possible. For example, instead of having one agent query five tools sequentially, wrap those tools in a single composite tool that executes them in parallel and returns a combined result. This avoids multiple round-trips and reduces orchestration overhead.

Monitoring and profiling are non-negotiable for sustained performance. Tools like OpenTelemetry or `httpx`'s built-in tracing can help you measure time spent in serialization, network IO, agent reasoning, and tool execution. You'll often find hotspots in unexpected places—like context construction routines or synchronous API calls blocking an async event loop.

Finally, tune timeouts and retries wisely. While we've discussed fault tolerance previously, too-aggressive retries or long timeouts can delay the entire chain. For latency-sensitive systems, it's better to fail fast and fallback than wait too long.

In short, performance tuning in MCP systems isn't about squeezing milliseconds in isolation—it's about optimizing the *flow* across clients, servers, tools, and agents. Trim payloads, cache aggressively, run warm, parallelize intelligently, and profile constantly. That's how you keep intelligent agents not only smart—but fast.

110

10.4 Documentation, Versioning, and Maintenance

Building and operating MCP-powered AI agents at scale demands a disciplined approach to documentation, version control, and ongoing maintenance. These are not just operational niceties—they are foundational to long-term reliability, developer productivity, and system evolution. The distributed and composable nature of MCP systems, where agents invoke tools and access resources via structured JSON-RPC calls, makes it critical to have clear records of what interfaces exist, what inputs they expect, and how they behave under different contexts.

Documentation should cover every exposed tool and resource, including parameters, expected inputs/outputs, error types, and authentication behaviors. A well-documented MCP server can be consumed by any compliant client, regardless of language or runtime, which is the core promise of MCP's interoperability. Auto-generating OpenAPI-like specs or markdown docs from code annotations is recommended, but always validate them against real usage. Annotate your functions with descriptions, edge case behavior, and version history to ensure that human developers and automated agents alike can make informed choices when invoking functionality.

Versioning is equally essential. In production systems, you must be able to evolve your server interfaces without breaking existing clients. Adopt semantic versioning (e.g., `v1.0.2`) for your MCP endpoints and explicitly expose version metadata during handshake or capability declaration phases. This allows older clients to continue functioning while newer clients opt into enhanced or modified behavior. Avoid introducing breaking changes without deprecating prior versions and setting clear timelines for their removal. Tag code versions in Git to match API versions and keep a changelog in your documentation that highlights breaking changes, new features, and security patches.

Maintenance includes regular audits of tool availability, performance bottlenecks, and agent usage patterns. Use observability tools discussed earlier to track which tools are popular, which are error-prone, and where latency is spiking. Establish a formal process for refactoring or retiring outdated tools, and provide migration notes for agents that depend on them. Even prompt templates should be version-controlled and tested under different LLM settings to detect performance regressions or hallucination shifts.

In summary, treating your MCP deployment as a living, evolving system—with rigorous documentation, careful versioning, and proactive maintenance—is the only sustainable way to scale intelligent agent architectures. These practices are what separate proof-of-concept agents from real-world systems capable of surviving continuous use and change.

10.5 Staying Current: Following MCP and LLM Evolutions

The Model Context Protocol (MCP) sits at the intersection of two rapidly evolving domains: structured agent communication protocols and foundation model capabilities. Staying current is not optional—it's a survival requirement for any team operating production-grade MCP agents. As LLMs advance in capabilities, input/output formats, and reasoning patterns, and as MCP itself iterates to support emerging use cases, your systems must evolve alongside them to remain relevant, efficient, and secure.

First, monitor updates to the MCP specification itself. While MCP is based on stable concepts like JSON-RPC 2.0, extensions and enhancements are being actively discussed and adopted in the ecosystem. These include things like capability negotiation schemas, streaming output support, dynamic function resolution, and richer error codes. Join community forums, working groups, or GitHub discussions related to MCP to stay informed. When new MCP features become available—such as function metadata introspection or multi-step invocation support—you'll want to assess their impact on your server/client codebases and rollout strategy.

Second, track evolutions in the LLMs that consume or power your agents. OpenAI, Anthropic, Cohere, Mistral, and others routinely release updated models with significant changes in behavior, token limits, function call fidelity, and system prompt expectations. These changes can directly affect how your agents interpret MCP responses or generate valid tool invocations. For example, a model upgrade might introduce better reasoning but stricter parsing of tool signatures, breaking workflows that previously worked. Maintain a sandbox environment to validate each new model version against your existing agent workflows and prompt templates before adopting it in production.

Third, invest in a modular system design that allows for easy upgrades. Use abstractions for your LLM interfaces and MCP bindings so that you can switch providers or protocol versions with minimal disruption. Implement configuration-based model routing so that different components of your system can adopt new models incrementally. Maintain backward compatibility in your tools and prompts, and use version headers to indicate what the client expects—ensuring you can safely support both legacy and cutting-edge consumers.

Lastly, schedule regular review cycles to audit your agents against the latest best practices. This includes checking for deprecated MCP features, redundant tools, insecure input handling patterns, or prompt techniques that are no longer effective given the current state of LLM reasoning. Treat your system not as a static deployment but as a living framework that requires care, iteration, and alignment with the broader AI ecosystem.

In short, staying current means building proactive awareness, testing carefully, upgrading selectively, and documenting continuously. The most effective MCP teams treat evolution not as disruption—but as opportunity for sharper, smarter, and more capable AI agents.

Chapter 11: Deploying MCP-Enabled Agents on AWS

11.1 Architecting MCP with Lambda, ECS, and API Gateway

Deploying MCP-enabled AI agents on AWS requires thoughtful orchestration of scalable compute, secure interfaces, and managed services. Three AWS building blocks—Lambda, ECS, and API Gateway—form a practical foundation for hosting MCP servers and exposing them to client agents across distributed environments. In this section, we'll walk through a real-world setup that maps the MCP server architecture onto AWS components, focusing on interoperability, deployment speed, and cost efficiency.

Let's start with **API Gateway**, which serves as the public entry point for all incoming MCP JSON-RPC requests. This service handles request routing, throttling, CORS, authentication (via API keys, IAM, or JWT authorizers), and request transformation. You define a REST or HTTP API Gateway endpoint that forwards requests directly to a compute backend—either AWS Lambda or a containerized MCP server running on ECS.

For lightweight, stateless MCP servers that only expose simple tools or respond with fast JSON payloads, **AWS Lambda** is ideal. You can implement your MCP server as a Python or Node.js function using the standard `jsonrpcserver` library or similar. For example, you might define a Lambda function that accepts a JSON-RPC request, parses the `method`, invokes a tool like `get_weather_report`, and returns the result in proper JSON-RPC format. Lambda handles concurrent execution, retries, and scaling automatically. You deploy your code using a ZIP package or container image, and connect it to API Gateway via an HTTP trigger.

For more complex scenarios—such as agents using persistent background processes, streaming contexts, or hosting large ML models—**Amazon ECS (Elastic Container Service)** with Fargate is a better fit. You build your MCP server as a Docker container using a framework like FastAPI, Flask, or Express, embed the necessary tool and resource logic, and deploy it to ECS. Fargate eliminates server management and allows you to scale based on

CPU, memory, or load. Use an ECS Service to maintain desired availability and configure your task definitions to run across availability zones.

Your architecture may even combine both: lightweight Lambda functions for stateless tools, and ECS services for heavier workloads. API Gateway can route different endpoints to different backends using route mappings. For example, `POST /invoke` might hit ECS, while `POST /healthcheck` triggers a quick Lambda.

Here's a simplified flow:

1. A remote MCP client sends a JSON-RPC `invoke` request to `https://api.yourdomain.com/invoke`.
2. API Gateway receives the call, enforces authorization, and forwards it to the ECS service.
3. The MCP server container validates the request, executes the method (e.g., `summarize_text`), and returns the response.
4. The client receives the structured result and continues its agent loop.

To ensure observability, integrate **CloudWatch Logs** with both Lambda and ECS for debugging and performance tracking. Use **AWS X-Ray** to trace call latency across services. For authentication, configure **IAM roles** for ECS tasks or API Gateway authorizers that verify tokens.

By modularizing your MCP deployment with these AWS services, you achieve a fault-tolerant, highly available, and cost-aware setup. Whether you're running a single-agent prototype or a multi-agent enterprise workflow, AWS provides the flexibility to scale MCP alongside your AI ambitions.

11.2 IAM, Network Security, and Fine-Grained Access

Securing MCP-powered agents in AWS environments requires a layered approach built around IAM, network controls, and principle of least privilege. At the heart of any secure MCP deployment is **Identity and Access Management (IAM)**—the framework that governs what components can interact, invoke methods, and access sensitive data. Alongside IAM, network-level controls such as security groups, VPCs, and subnets ensure that MCP servers and clients operate within clearly defined trust boundaries, reducing the risk of unauthorized communication or data exfiltration.

When deploying MCP servers on **AWS ECS** or **Lambda**, each component must assume an IAM role that defines its permissions. For example, an MCP server running in ECS should have a task execution role allowing it to pull images from Amazon ECR, write logs to CloudWatch, and optionally access other AWS services like S3 or DynamoDB if those are used as part of MCP resources. This role is defined in the ECS task definition. In parallel, if you're using an MCP client running as a Lambda function that needs to call `invoke` methods via API Gateway, you should attach a separate IAM role to that Lambda function that restricts access to only the allowed endpoints, with permissions limited to specific stages and methods using IAM policy conditions.

Next, **API Gateway authorization** plays a key role in controlling which clients can reach MCP endpoints. For public-facing APIs, use **JWT authorizers** or custom Lambda authorizers that inspect access tokens, verify scopes or claims, and enforce user-specific permissions. For internal-only agents, **IAM-based authorization** can be used, which requires the client to sign requests with AWS Signature V4 and ensures that only trusted principals within your AWS account can make requests. For example, an MCP client could use boto3 or AWS SDKs to generate a signed POST request to an API Gateway endpoint, and the server would verify the caller's role before executing any methods.

On the networking side, if your MCP server runs in ECS, it should be placed within a **private subnet** inside a **VPC**. Use **security groups** to tightly control which IP ranges or services can reach the containerized MCP service. For instance, only an internal API Gateway or an AWS Load Balancer in a public subnet should be able to access the MCP server's listener port. Outbound calls (e.g. fetching external context) can be routed through a **NAT gateway**. For Lambda, network control is achieved by assigning the function to a VPC and configuring its subnet and security group access.

Let's walk through a practical example. Suppose you're deploying a secure financial document analysis agent. The MCP server is hosted in ECS and exposes a `process_document` tool that accesses encrypted PDFs in S3. The ECS task runs with an IAM role that grants read access to the `s3://confidential-docs-bucket`, and only allows execution of specific actions like `s3:GetObject` on objects with a certain prefix (`financial/`). API Gateway is configured with a JWT authorizer that validates the identity and organization of the calling client. The client must present a signed token issued by your IdP. The ECS service is deployed into a VPC with restricted ingress, allowing traffic only from API Gateway's CIDR range, and logs

116

every invocation to CloudWatch with request metadata scrubbed and anonymized for compliance.

By enforcing this security posture with IAM boundaries, scoped permissions, and network segmentation, you ensure that even if an agent misbehaves, it cannot step beyond its designated role or data domain. Fine-grained access is not just about safety—it's the foundation of scalable, compliant, and trustworthy agentic systems. This architecture scales cleanly as you grow your network of MCP agents while maintaining centralized control and auditability over every interaction.

11.3 Using S3, Bedrock, and EventBridge with Agents

Integrating AWS services such as Amazon S3, Bedrock, and EventBridge into MCP-powered agents enables a powerful orchestration pattern for real-time document processing, model invocation, and event-driven workflows. Each service complements a different layer of the agent's capability—S3 for storage and data access, Bedrock for model inference, and EventBridge for signaling and automation.

When using **Amazon S3**, agents can treat it as an MCP resource that either stores prompt inputs (like uploaded documents or structured files) or captures outputs (like summaries, transcripts, or generated insights). The MCP server should expose a resource method like `get_s3_object` or `upload_result_to_s3`, internally using the AWS SDK to interact with buckets. The resource must sanitize paths, validate permissions, and log all interactions for auditability. A typical use case involves an end-user uploading a PDF into `s3://mcp-agent-docs/uploads/`, and the agent retrieving it during execution for processing. The S3 object URL and key can be passed as context or metadata in the prompt payload to ensure reproducibility and traceability.

Amazon Bedrock can be treated as a dynamic backend for your agent's reasoning or generation tasks. Instead of hardwiring a specific model (like Claude or Titan), you can use an MCP tool called `invoke_bedrock_model` that abstracts Bedrock API calls. The MCP tool accepts the model ID (e.g. `anthropic.claude-v2`) and a prompt or input payload. Internally, it handles API keys, rate limits, and error responses from Bedrock. This allows your agents to flexibly call multiple foundation models, choosing the best one for the task at runtime. For example, a summarization agent may default to

Claude for long documents, but fall back to Titan for faster short-form responses.

To illustrate this, consider an MCP server exposing the following tool:

```
def invoke_bedrock_model(model_id: str, prompt: str) -> str:
    response = bedrock_client.invoke_model(
        modelId=model_id,
        body=json.dumps({"prompt": prompt, "max_tokens":
500})
    )
    return json.loads(response['body'].read())['completion']
```

This server-side tool is then registered in your MCP manifest and becomes callable from any compliant agent client.

Finally, **Amazon EventBridge** provides the glue layer for event-driven chaining. You can configure an EventBridge rule to trigger an MCP client Lambda function when a new object is added to a monitored S3 bucket. This Lambda, acting as an MCP client, connects to your MCP server, calls the process_document tool, and stores the result back in S3 or sends it to another service. EventBridge can also be used to notify external systems (e.g., Slack, SNS, or a downstream workflow) once an agent completes its task, using the PutEvents API to publish structured outputs.

Here's a real-world scenario: a financial compliance pipeline where analysts upload regulatory PDFs to a secure S3 bucket. EventBridge detects the upload and triggers a Lambda MCP client, which calls the MCP server's summarize_pdf tool. That tool internally uses Bedrock to summarize, stores the result back to S3, and emits an EventBridge notification that triggers a follow-up review step by a human-in-the-loop system.

This architecture enables scalable, low-latency, and secure workflows where context lives in S3, intelligence flows through Bedrock, and control is maintained via EventBridge. Each service integrates seamlessly with the MCP pattern, allowing you to build agentic systems that are modular, event-driven, and production-ready.

11.4 Scaling Techniques and Auto-Healing Deployments

Scaling MCP-enabled agent systems in the cloud—especially on AWS—involves designing resilient infrastructure that can handle spikes in demand, recover gracefully from failures, and support concurrent agent sessions without bottlenecks. The Model Context Protocol (MCP), with its decoupled architecture of clients, servers, and tools/resources, naturally lends itself to cloud-native scalability patterns. However, to make the most of it, you must integrate key AWS features such as auto-scaling groups, container orchestration, health checks, and load balancers.

At the core of scalable deployment is the **MCP Server**, typically containerized and hosted on Amazon ECS (Elastic Container Service) with Fargate or EC2 launch types. ECS allows you to define a task definition that includes your MCP server container, environment variables (e.g., API keys, model endpoints), logging configuration (e.g., CloudWatch), and port mappings. You then deploy this task into a service behind an **Application Load Balancer (ALB)**. The ALB routes incoming JSON-RPC or HTTP POST requests to the appropriate container instance based on path or host rules.

To enable **scaling**, you configure **Service Auto Scaling** on ECS. This lets your service automatically adjust the number of running MCP server tasks based on metrics such as CPU utilization or request throughput. For example, if each container can handle 50 concurrent requests and the system receives a surge of 500, ECS can spin up 10 containers in response—without manual intervention. This ensures horizontal scalability without affecting latency.

In parallel, **Auto-Healing** ensures reliability by continuously monitoring the health of each MCP container. AWS offers two main mechanisms for this. First, ECS itself performs task-level health checks based on your container's heartbeat (e.g., an `/healthz` endpoint that returns 200 OK). If the container becomes unresponsive, ECS automatically kills and replaces the task. Second, if you use an ALB, it can also perform target group health checks. These can detect broken deployments, memory leaks, or dependency failures and deregister unhealthy instances from routing.

For advanced deployments, many teams leverage **AWS CloudWatch Alarms** to track deeper health metrics such as memory consumption, container restarts, and tool execution failures. These alarms can trigger **AWS Lambda functions** that notify admins, execute failover strategies, or initiate rollbacks if a bad deployment causes agent downtime.

In scenarios where agents rely on asynchronous job handling or long-running tasks (e.g., batch processing via MCP tools), **Amazon SQS** and **AWS Step Functions** can be used to offload queue-based workloads. MCP tools can enqueue requests for downstream processing, and worker containers can independently scale based on queue depth.

As an example, suppose your MCP server includes a `transcribe_audio` tool that calls a heavy external service. Rather than process this synchronously, the MCP tool writes a message to an SQS queue. A separate ECS service reads from the queue, processes the request, and posts the result back to an S3 bucket. This decouples real-time prompts from compute-intensive backend tasks and improves fault isolation.

In production deployments, you should also enable **ECS Service Discovery** and DNS-based routing using AWS Cloud Map. This ensures that MCP clients running across different subnets or regions can discover available MCP servers without hardcoded IPs or manual registration.

In summary, scaling and auto-healing MCP deployments require a layered approach: container orchestration for elasticity, load balancing for routing, health checks for resilience, and observability for proactive intervention. By combining these AWS features with the inherent modularity of MCP, you can build robust agent systems that stay responsive, recover from failures, and grow dynamically with user demand.

11.5 AWS Budgets and Monitoring for Cost Control

Deploying MCP-enabled AI agents on AWS requires not just reliable architecture and scalable compute—but vigilant cost oversight. Given the modular nature of MCP systems, costs can accrue from multiple AWS services including Lambda, ECS, API Gateway, Bedrock, S3, and EventBridge. To prevent uncontrolled expenses, it's essential to implement budget controls, automated alerts, and usage monitoring right from the start.

Begin by configuring **AWS Budgets**, a service that lets you define cost thresholds and usage limits for your entire MCP deployment or specific services like Lambda or Bedrock inference. For example, if your architecture uses Bedrock to invoke Claude or Titan for certain agent tasks, set a monthly spending limit on that service. Define alerts that notify via SNS or email when 80% or 100% of the threshold is reached. Pair this with **Cost Anomaly Detection** to flag unexpected spikes, which may indicate inefficiencies or misuse of tools.

For real-time observability, use **Amazon CloudWatch** dashboards to track metrics like invocation count, execution duration, and error rates for individual MCP Tools or Resources. Enable **CloudWatch Logs Insights** to run queries across logs and correlate spikes in usage with specific agents or functions. For instance, if a particular Resource is consuming more compute time than expected, logs can help you identify inefficient code or frequent retries.

Also enable **AWS Cost Explorer**, which gives you a granular view of where your budget is going—broken down by service, linked accounts, or resource tags. This is particularly useful when allocating cost ownership across different agent roles, environments (dev/test/prod), or external tool integrations.

To go a step further, configure **automated actions with AWS Budgets**. For example, you can throttle API Gateway usage or disable certain Lambda functions once a critical budget limit is exceeded. This prevents runaway spending in case of logic errors or denial-of-wallet attacks.

In summary, combining AWS Budgets, CloudWatch, and Cost Explorer provides a robust framework for ensuring that your MCP-enabled agents operate within financial constraints. By actively monitoring and adjusting based on usage patterns, you'll preserve both technical agility and fiscal discipline—key ingredients for scaling responsibly in the cloud.

Chapter 12: Azure Deployment for MCP-Powered Agents

12.1 Functions, App Services, and Kubernetes on Azure

Deploying MCP-powered agents on Azure requires a thoughtful mapping of protocol components—tools, resources, and context handlers—to scalable cloud-native services. Azure offers multiple compute options suitable for different stages of agent system maturity, from prototyping with serverless functions to production-grade orchestration with AKS (Azure Kubernetes Service).

For lightweight or event-driven agents, **Azure Functions** provide a seamless way to host MCP tools and resources as stateless endpoints. Each function can expose a discrete capability—for example, an MCP tool that calculates financial risk or a resource that retrieves market data. These functions are triggered via HTTP requests following the JSON-RPC format, and Azure's consumption plan ensures you pay only for the execution time. During development, you can locally test these functions using the Azure Functions Core Tools before deploying them to the cloud.

When you need a bit more control over runtime or want to combine multiple tools behind a single domain, **Azure App Service** becomes ideal. MCP servers—often running as Flask or FastAPI apps—can be deployed on App Service with easy CI/CD integration via GitHub Actions or Azure DevOps. You get built-in features like auto-scaling, managed SSL, staging environments, and diagnostic logging without needing to manage infrastructure. MCP endpoints running under App Service benefit from predictable routing and can be tied into virtual networks for secure internal agent communication.

For production environments requiring horizontal scaling, custom runtimes, or containerized workloads, **Azure Kubernetes Service (AKS)** is the most powerful option. With AKS, you can containerize your MCP server along with context processors, vector databases, and auxiliary services, all orchestrated under one cluster. This setup allows multi-agent systems to run in parallel with persistent volumes, GPU-enabled nodes (for inference backends), and service meshes like Istio for traffic control. MCP clients—like LangChain agents—can invoke these tools via internal load balancers, reducing latency and ensuring secure communication within the cluster.

A practical example: suppose you're deploying a context-aware support assistant for a healthcare provider. You can run real-time symptom triage logic as an Azure Function, host the main MCP server on App Service (with private access to internal EHR APIs), and offload data-intensive processing to AKS using a dedicated node pool.

In summary, Azure gives you a flexible progression path for deploying MCP-powered systems—starting from lightweight prototypes on Functions, moving through App Service for mid-scale integration, and ultimately achieving scalable, secure, and production-ready deployments on Kubernetes. This layered deployment strategy aligns with the modular architecture MCP promotes, enabling developers to focus on agent capabilities rather than infrastructure complexity.

12.2 Using Azure OpenAI and Cognitive Services

Integrating Azure OpenAI and Cognitive Services with MCP-powered agents opens the door to intelligent, context-aware systems that leverage the full spectrum of Microsoft's AI capabilities—securely and at scale. MCP's modular architecture makes it an ideal fit for bridging LLM-based reasoning with Azure's extensive suite of AI APIs, ranging from natural language to vision and speech.

To begin, Azure OpenAI provides hosted access to powerful LLMs like GPT-4 and GPT-3.5 under enterprise-grade compliance. An MCP agent can invoke Azure OpenAI endpoints either as a Tool—exposing functionality such as summarization, sentiment analysis, or structured output generation—or as a full agent backend. Using the `azure-openai` Python client or standard HTTPS requests, your MCP client can format a JSON-RPC call like `llm.summarize` or `llm.answer`, and route it through a custom Azure endpoint secured with API keys and identity-based access (via Azure AD if needed). You define these tools within your MCP server's tool manifest, ensuring every interaction stays observable and traceable.

Here's a simplified real-world scenario. Let's say you're building an agent that helps legal teams review lengthy documents. You expose an MCP tool `extract.key_points` which, under the hood, formats the user prompt and forwards it to Azure OpenAI for semantic summarization. Meanwhile, a paired `search.case_law` resource queries a private database indexed in Azure Cognitive Search. Both the OpenAI model and the search index operate independently, but MCP allows them to be orchestrated as part of a seamless multi-turn dialogue flow.

Now consider Azure Cognitive Services, which includes APIs for language understanding (LUIS), speech-to-text, image classification, OCR, and more. MCP resources can act as adapters that wrap these APIs. For instance, you might expose `resource.ocr_invoice` to extract fields from scanned receipts using the Azure Form Recognizer. Or `resource.speech_to_text` might use Azure Speech Services to transcribe user input before passing it into a prompt pipeline. Each of these is defined in your server's resource configuration and served over a well-defined JSON-RPC method.

In production, combining Azure OpenAI and Cognitive Services through MCP enables multi-modal and multi-intent systems. A healthcare bot could process voice input, extract symptoms using language models, and retrieve structured patient data—all mediated by MCP to ensure component separation, traceability, and logging. This architecture not only improves observability but allows individual services to evolve independently.

Ultimately, by treating Azure's AI offerings as composable elements and exposing them through well-defined MCP tools and resources, developers can craft intelligent agents that are secure, auditable, and robust—suitable for real-world use across enterprise domains.

12.3 Secure Access to SQL and Blob Storage

Accessing SQL databases and Blob Storage securely from MCP-powered agents is critical when designing context-rich applications that require structured or large-scale unstructured data. In a typical enterprise scenario, agents must not only retrieve and manipulate data, but do so within strict security, auditing, and permission boundaries. Azure provides fine-grained identity, encryption, and networking mechanisms that integrate seamlessly with MCP's resource model.

Let's begin with SQL. In Azure, SQL Server or Azure SQL Database can be accessed by MCP resources acting as context providers. For example, you might define a method like `resource.customer_profile.fetch` that queries user information based on an email address or ID. This resource internally connects to a SQL database using a secure connection string—either stored as an environment variable or retrieved via Azure Key Vault at runtime. The MCP server handles the incoming JSON-RPC request, securely opens a database connection using the `pyodbc` or `asyncpg` driver, executes the query, and returns results in structured JSON format.

Security best practices here include using Azure Managed Identity when your MCP server is hosted within Azure App Services or Azure Kubernetes Service (AKS). This allows the MCP server to authenticate to the database without storing secrets, using Azure Active Directory (AAD) under the hood. Additionally, firewall rules should restrict access to trusted IPs or VNETs only.

Now consider Blob Storage—useful for unstructured data such as logs, transcripts, documents, or images. You might expose a resource method like `resource.files.get_latest_transcript`, which fetches the latest uploaded conversation log for a user. Internally, this method connects to an Azure Storage Account and reads from a designated container. With the `azure-storage-blob` Python SDK, the resource can authenticate via a connection string, SAS token, or again via Managed Identity if the server is running in Azure.

To ensure security and compliance, it is recommended to enforce HTTPS-only access on your Storage Account, enable soft delete and immutable storage (for audit logs), and set appropriate access control levels (e.g., private container access with role-based authorization). When integrating Blob access within prompts or tool results, the MCP server should ensure content is scrubbed of sensitive metadata and sanitized before use.

For real-world integration, imagine a legal document review agent that fetches scanned contracts from Blob Storage, passes them through a Form Recognizer tool for key data extraction, and stores results in SQL. All these operations are modular MCP methods—`resource.blob.fetch_contract`, `tool.ocr.parse`, and `resource.db.write_summary`—executed in a secure, orchestrated sequence. Role-based access can control which users or agent personas are permitted to access which resources, enforced through your server's auth middleware.

In summary, secure access to Azure SQL and Blob Storage in MCP agents hinges on well-scoped resources, secretless authentication via Managed Identity, network isolation, and encrypted communication. MCP provides the abstraction layer that decouples business logic from storage infrastructure, making it easier to build scalable, composable, and security-first AI systems.

12.4 Scaling with Azure Monitor and Insights

As MCP-based AI agents mature from development into production environments, scaling and observability become paramount. Azure Monitor, alongside Application Insights and Log Analytics, provides the tooling backbone necessary for diagnosing issues, understanding performance bottlenecks, and dynamically scaling services that power MCP servers and clients. These services are especially useful when orchestrating complex, context-aware agents across distributed cloud components.

To begin with, Azure Monitor offers a unified platform for collecting metrics, logs, and traces from all your Azure resources. When deploying MCP servers—whether on App Services, Azure Functions, or Kubernetes— integrating with Azure Monitor allows you to track CPU usage, memory consumption, response time, request rates, and internal failures. For example, if your MCP tool endpoints (like `tool.summarize.text`) experience sudden latency spikes due to high concurrency, Azure Monitor can automatically alert you and trigger auto-scaling rules defined in App Service Plans or AKS node pools.

Application Insights extends this capability by capturing deeper telemetry about individual requests, exceptions, dependencies (like SQL queries or blob reads), and user-defined custom events. When an MCP resource such as `resource.financials.get_report` is queried, Application Insights records the time it takes for the database to respond, logs the full stack trace if an exception occurs, and visualizes the trace using a dependency map. By embedding lightweight telemetry SDKs in your MCP server code, developers can add custom spans and log structured context such as agent IDs, session hashes, or prompt metadata.

Here's a practical walkthrough. Suppose you're running an MCP server on Azure App Services with several exposed endpoints for AI-powered financial recommendations. You enable Application Insights and add a logging hook inside each JSON-RPC method. When a client sends a request to `tool.recommend.portfolio`, your handler logs input size, model name, round-trip latency, and response payload summary. This data is sent to Application Insights in real-time. If latency crosses a threshold or if errors rise above a baseline, Azure Monitor triggers an alert. The alert, in turn, might scale up the App Service Plan from 2 to 4 instances and notify your DevOps team via Azure DevOps or Microsoft Teams integration.

Furthermore, Log Analytics offers a queryable interface to analyze the data pipeline across agents. For example, you might write a Kusto Query Language (KQL) query to determine the 95th percentile latency across all prompt chains that invoke both `tool.embedding.encode` and `resource.docs.search`. This gives engineering teams the ability to pinpoint which resource combinations degrade under load, and where optimizations—such as prompt size reduction or cache injection—should be focused.

To complete the loop, Azure supports autoscale profiles based on CPU thresholds, custom metrics, or schedule-based patterns. For AKS-based deployments, the Kubernetes Metrics Server and Horizontal Pod Autoscaler can work with Azure Monitor to scale MCP workloads dynamically. In a production setting, this allows your AI agents to serve thousands of concurrent requests with consistent responsiveness, while keeping infrastructure costs under control.

In summary, Azure Monitor and Insights are foundational for scaling MCP-powered systems responsibly. They provide the observability and control plane that developers and operations teams need to ensure performance, reliability, and cost-efficiency across AI-driven services. As your agents grow more intelligent and interconnected, so too must your approach to diagnostics and dynamic scaling—and Azure offers the necessary building blocks to make that seamless.

12.5 Billing and Optimization Strategies

Deploying MCP-powered agents on Azure introduces a range of flexible and scalable options, but with that flexibility comes the responsibility of cost management. Understanding how your infrastructure components are billed—and how to optimize their usage—can make the difference between an efficient AI architecture and an unsustainable one. This section focuses on practical billing strategies and actionable optimization techniques tailored specifically to MCP deployments.

Azure's billing model charges based on consumption, which includes compute time, storage, networking, and any specialized services such as Azure OpenAI, Cognitive Services, or Azure SQL. For example, if your

MCP server is hosted on Azure Functions in a Consumption Plan, you're billed by the number of executions and the compute duration per invocation. On the other hand, App Services and AKS (Azure Kubernetes Service) follow a more static pricing tier or node-based model, where you pay for the resources regardless of use.

To begin optimizing, start with **Azure Cost Management and Billing**, which provides dashboards and forecasting tools to help visualize spend by service, region, and resource group. You can filter to isolate costs specifically related to your MCP infrastructure. For instance, if you're running multiple MCP tools for different teams—each deployed as separate Azure Functions—you can tag each resource by function (e.g., `mcp-summarizer`, `mcp-searcher`) and analyze their individual cost footprints.

One effective strategy is **rightsizing**. In early development, it's common to over-provision App Service Plans or AKS node pools. Review the actual usage metrics from Azure Monitor and scale down underutilized plans. For example, if your App Service averages less than 20% CPU utilization even during peak hours, downgrading to a lower pricing tier or switching to a Consumption Plan for functions can save hundreds of dollars monthly.

Cold start latency for serverless deployments can affect both performance and cost. If an MCP agent calls a tool that triggers a cold-starting Azure Function, the delay can propagate through your agent's workflow, increasing token usage and client wait time. To mitigate this, consider using the **Premium Plan** for Functions, which pre-warms instances, or schedule periodic warm-up invocations during expected activity windows.

When your MCP agents use **Azure OpenAI or Cognitive Services**, keep track of API call frequency and prompt sizes. Each token sent or received has a cost, so minimizing verbose system prompts and using compact context representations can drastically reduce usage. Also, leverage features like caching intermediate results or encoding embeddings offline when possible, especially when the same data is frequently requested.

In storage-heavy use cases—for instance, when MCP Resources pull structured content from **Blob Storage** or **Azure SQL**—optimize data access patterns. Use **tiered storage** for less-frequently accessed data (cool/archive tiers), enable **Geo-redundancy** only when required by compliance, and compress data before upload. With SQL, configure auto-pausing and auto-scaling for serverless instances so you're not billed during idle hours.

You can also automate cost control using **Budgets and Alerts**. Set a monthly threshold for your MCP deployment resource group, and configure automated actions if spending approaches the limit—such as scaling down services, disabling non-critical components, or triggering administrative notifications.

In closing, effective billing and optimization for MCP deployments on Azure requires a combination of architectural awareness, proactive monitoring, and smart automation. By leveraging Azure's built-in tools and aligning your infrastructure with usage patterns, you can build intelligent, context-aware agents that not only scale but do so economically. This financial discipline is crucial for teams transitioning from prototypes to enterprise-grade, cost-effective MCP systems.

Chapter 13: Deploying on Google Cloud Platform

13.1 GKE, Cloud Run, and Cloud Functions Setup

Google Cloud Platform (GCP) offers a flexible and scalable environment for deploying MCP-powered agents. Whether you're building a small serverless tool or orchestrating a complex multi-agent system, GCP provides three key deployment primitives to choose from: Google Kubernetes Engine (GKE), Cloud Run, and Cloud Functions. Each option supports different use cases depending on your performance, scaling, and development preferences.

Google Kubernetes Engine (GKE) is the most powerful and customizable option, ideal for production-grade MCP deployments where control over container orchestration, networking, and persistent volumes is essential. You begin by containerizing your MCP server—typically a Python FastAPI or Node.js service exposing JSON-RPC endpoints—and then deploying it as a Kubernetes deployment. The GKE cluster handles scheduling, health checks, autoscaling, and rolling updates. You'll also define Kubernetes `Service` and `Ingress` resources to expose the MCP server via a stable IP or load balancer. For example, if your MCP tool needs to maintain in-memory state across calls or depends on GPU inference, GKE gives you the operational flexibility required.

However, for lighter, stateless workloads such as individual MCP tools or prompt-handling endpoints, **Cloud Run** offers a serverless container runtime that drastically simplifies deployment. You build your container image (with a Dockerfile) and deploy it directly from a container registry like Artifact Registry or Docker Hub. Cloud Run automatically handles scaling based on request volume, including down to zero when idle, and integrates with Cloud IAM for fine-grained access control. This makes it a strong candidate for prompt-focused MCP endpoints or resource servers that respond to HTTP calls and can cold-start quickly.

Cloud Functions is another serverless option, designed for small, event-driven workloads. It's especially effective when used in conjunction with MCP resources that are triggered by file uploads (e.g., via Cloud Storage),

Pub/Sub messages, or time-based schedules. For example, you might write a lightweight function that formats financial data pulled from BigQuery, caches the result in Firestore, and exposes it to your MCP agent via a simple GET route. While Cloud Functions has tighter constraints around execution time and resource availability compared to Cloud Run or GKE, its tight integration with GCP services makes it valuable for isolated utility tasks.

In terms of setup, all three options follow a similar high-level workflow:

1. **Develop and test your MCP server or component locally**.
2. **Containerize your app** (except with first-class support for Python or Node.js, Cloud Functions doesn't require a Docker container).
3. **Deploy via `gcloud` CLI or web console**, configuring environment variables (like auth tokens, prompt templates, or model endpoints) through secure means such as Secret Manager or Cloud Config.

You'll also want to integrate **Cloud Logging and Cloud Monitoring** for real-time observability. Each of these platforms emits traceable logs that you can filter by label, resource name, or error level to debug agent behavior and measure performance.

To secure your MCP endpoints, you should use **Identity-Aware Proxy (IAP)** or **JWT-based authentication**, depending on whether your tools are public-facing or internally consumed by other services. For example, an agent hosted on Cloud Run can require a signed ID token to access a sensitive resource, like a finance data summarizer, ensuring only authorized clients can trigger actions.

In summary, GCP offers multiple deployment paths depending on your architecture goals. Use GKE when you need full control and scalability; use Cloud Run for quick, stateless deployments of MCP servers; and use Cloud Functions for modular, event-triggered components. Each path integrates seamlessly with GCP's developer ecosystem, providing the building blocks needed for secure, performant, and scalable MCP-enabled AI agent systems.

13.2 Using Vertex AI and BigQuery with MCP Agents

Integrating Vertex AI and BigQuery with MCP agents allows you to build intelligent, context-aware systems capable of real-time reasoning, data analysis, and decision-making at scale. This combination brings together the strengths of Google's powerful model serving infrastructure and its fully managed data warehouse, enabling your MCP-powered agents to reason over enterprise-grade datasets with low latency.

Let's begin by understanding how Vertex AI and BigQuery fit into the MCP workflow. Vertex AI serves as the inference backend—where models like PaLM, Gemini, or custom-trained LLMs are hosted—while BigQuery acts as the contextual data layer, providing structured information to enhance prompt grounding or tool execution. The Model Context Protocol bridges these systems, allowing agents to issue structured `tool.call` or `resource.get` requests, receive data from BigQuery, format it using prompt templates, and invoke Vertex-hosted models—all in one seamless pipeline.

Here's a hands-on example that demonstrates how you might implement this integration.

Start by building a **MCP tool** that queries BigQuery for customer purchase history. You can use the Python `google-cloud-bigquery` client to execute parameterized SQL queries. The tool's implementation must expose a callable JSON-RPC method such as `purchase_history.lookup`, taking `customer_id` as input and returning a summary of results:

```python
from google.cloud import bigquery

def purchase_history_lookup(params):
    client = bigquery.Client()
    query = """
        SELECT product_name, total_spent, last_purchase_date
        FROM `myproject.sales.customers`
        WHERE customer_id = @customer_id
        LIMIT 10
    """
    job_config = bigquery.QueryJobConfig(

query_parameters=[bigquery.ScalarQueryParameter("customer_id"
, "STRING", params["customer_id"])]
    )
    result = client.query(query,
job_config=job_config).result()
    return [{"product": row.product_name, "spent":
row.total_spent, "last": row.last_purchase_date.isoformat()}
for row in result]
```

Once the BigQuery integration is complete, your MCP server can register this as a tool callable by any agent connected to the server. You'll also want to add response formatting logic to transform the output into natural language or structured summaries before passing it into a model invocation.

On the model side, **Vertex AI PaLM or Gemini models** can be called using the `google-cloud-aiplatform` library. The prompt that receives BigQuery output can be dynamically filled using a registered prompt template, then sent to the model for inference:

```python
from vertexai.language_models import TextGenerationModel

def generate_response(prompt):
    model = TextGenerationModel.from_pretrained("text-bison")
    response = model.predict(prompt, temperature=0.2,
max_output_tokens=256)
    return response.text
```

Now, tie it all together in your MCP client (e.g., a LangChain agent or a custom frontend). It issues a `tool.call` to retrieve structured context from BigQuery, uses that as input for a prompt, then performs a `tool.invoke` to send it to the Vertex model for final generation.

Security and access control are critical here. Use **Service Accounts with minimal IAM scopes**, ensuring that only necessary permissions (e.g., BigQuery read-only, Vertex prediction access) are granted. Store credentials securely via Secret Manager or use Workload Identity Federation for zero-secret deployments.

For observability, log both the BigQuery requests and the model invocation payloads into **Cloud Logging**, and use **Vertex AI Insights** for monitoring token usage, latency, and model output patterns. This helps maintain traceability and optimize cost-performance trade-offs.

In summary, the integration of Vertex AI and BigQuery into an MCP-based agent architecture unlocks the ability to reason over live datasets and generate intelligent responses. BigQuery provides rich context, while Vertex AI supplies language understanding and synthesis—glued together by a structured protocol that supports modular, reusable, and scalable agent design.

13.3 IAM and Context Isolation with GCP

In deploying MCP-enabled agents on Google Cloud Platform (GCP), one of the most crucial architectural concerns is ensuring tight security controls through Identity and Access Management (IAM) and effective isolation of context between different agent sessions or tenants. Without these guardrails, even the most advanced AI workflows become vulnerable to data leaks, privilege escalation, or operational conflicts. GCP offers robust primitives that, when integrated properly with MCP, provide a scalable foundation for secure multi-agent deployments.

At the core of secure deployments is GCP IAM, which governs **who has access to what** across your cloud resources. In an MCP deployment, you'll typically need to secure three categories: BigQuery datasets or external APIs used in tools/resources, Vertex AI models used for inference, and the MCP services themselves (running on Cloud Functions, Cloud Run, or GKE). The best practice is to **assign each MCP component its own service account**, with the **least privilege** principle enforced.

For example, if your MCP tool needs to access BigQuery but not Vertex AI, you can create a service account `mcp-tool-bq-access@project.iam.gserviceaccount.com` and bind only the `BigQuery Data Viewer` role to it. This isolates permissions by function, and if compromised, limits blast radius. These roles are bound using IAM policy bindings:

```
gcloud projects add-iam-policy-binding my-project-id \
   --member="serviceAccount:mcp-tool-bq-
access@project.iam.gserviceaccount.com" \
   --role="roles/bigquery.dataViewer"
```

Now turning to **context isolation**, this becomes especially important when multiple users or agents interact with the same MCP server. In this setting, context might refer to prompt history, session identifiers, external data state, or real-time inputs stored in shared resources like GCS or Firestore. The protocol must treat each session as a discrete unit of authority. To enforce this, you can combine **Workload Identity Pools** with **per-session temporary tokens** to make sure access is scoped at runtime.

One technique involves generating a signed token per session with metadata on agent ID, allowed tool scope, and TTL. The MCP server validates the token before fulfilling a request and uses its claims to restrict which tools or resources the agent may access. For example, an agent with context limited to project A cannot retrieve data scoped to project B.

GCP also provides **VPC Service Controls** for further boundary protection between services. If your MCP system spans sensitive data environments, using VPC SC helps prevent data exfiltration between contexts, particularly when agents query external APIs or fetch resources. Additionally, using **resource-level access policies** on GCS buckets, Firestore collections, or BigQuery datasets ensures only authorized service accounts can read/write context.

For real-time runtime enforcement, your MCP components can log and audit context-related actions using **Cloud Audit Logs**, storing the identity of the caller, the method invoked, and the target resource. This audit trail enables compliance verification and post-incident analysis, particularly useful for applications subject to HIPAA, SOC 2, or ISO 27001 standards.

In summary, IAM and context isolation in GCP are not optional luxuries—they're foundational components of a secure, production-grade MCP deployment. By separating service accounts, applying least privilege roles, using signed tokens to gate resource access, and maintaining audit logs for traceability, you ensure that your MCP agents remain secure, compliant, and reliable—regardless of how complex or multi-tenant your system becomes.

13.4 Real-Time Monitoring with Cloud Ops Suite

As MCP-powered AI agents scale across Google Cloud Platform, real-time monitoring becomes essential—not just for debugging and operational visibility, but also for ensuring the reliability, performance, and trustworthiness of autonomous workflows. Google Cloud's **Cloud Operations Suite**—formerly Stackdriver—offers an integrated observability stack that includes **Cloud Monitoring**, **Cloud Logging**, and **Cloud Trace**, which are perfectly suited to monitoring MCP servers, tools, and clients in production.

To begin with, every MCP component deployed on GCP—whether it's a Cloud Function exposing an MCP Tool, a Cloud Run service acting as a server, or a GKE pod running contextual resource handlers—automatically emits logs and metrics when correctly configured. These logs include invocation data, latency, error messages, request payloads, and more. You can stream this telemetry directly to **Cloud Logging**, where you can create **custom log-based metrics** to track specific events in the MCP lifecycle.

For example, to track how many times a specific MCP tool like `context.search` is invoked, you can define a log-based metric with a filter like:

```
resource.type="cloud_run_revision"
logName="projects/my-
project/logs/run.googleapis.com%2Fstdout"
textPayload:"method":"context.search"
```

This metric can then be visualized in **Cloud Monitoring Dashboards**, where you might also overlay CPU usage, memory, request count, and response latency. MCP agents often involve chaining several tools together—these dashboards help detect bottlenecks, slow tools, or resource constraints across the workflow.

Moreover, **Cloud Trace** becomes invaluable when you need to analyze latency across distributed MCP systems. Each request to an MCP server, especially when invoking tools that interact with external APIs or databases, can be traced end-to-end. By instrumenting your MCP components with OpenTelemetry (supported in most GCP services), you enable trace correlation between invocations, making it possible to isolate slow dependencies or understand cascading delays in context propagation.

For example, if an MCP server receives a JSON-RPC call to execute `report.generate`, Cloud Trace will show whether the delay came from tool execution, downstream database queries, or the LLM response generation itself. This level of granularity is crucial for production-readiness.

Alerting is also a core feature. You can set up alerting policies on any collected metric—say, if the error rate on a tool exceeds 5% over 5 minutes, or if CPU utilization on your Cloud Run service spikes beyond 80%. These alerts can trigger notifications via email, Slack, PagerDuty, or custom webhooks. This ensures your operations team can respond quickly to failures or performance degradations.

Additionally, **Cloud Profiler** helps optimize performance by showing CPU and memory usage down to function-level granularity in your Python- or Node-based MCP code. It's especially useful when an MCP tool is computationally intensive and you need to optimize code for performance or cost.

Lastly, all collected metrics and logs are **retained** and queryable via **Cloud Logging Explorer** and **Cloud Monitoring Metrics Explorer**. This makes it easy to perform historical analysis, diagnose post-incident root causes, and even export data to BigQuery for further analysis or dashboards with Looker Studio.

In summary, the Cloud Ops Suite provides everything needed to run MCP-based AI agents with production-grade observability. By leveraging its native integration with GCP services, structured logging, log-based metrics, end-to-end tracing, and intelligent alerting, you can ensure your MCP infrastructure remains visible, accountable, and scalable—key pillars for mission-critical AI deployments.

13.5 Cost-Effective Deployments on GCP

Deploying MCP-powered agents on Google Cloud Platform offers flexibility and performance, but controlling cost is just as critical as ensuring reliability. As workloads scale and multiple MCP servers, tools, and resources interact in real-time, developers must make architectural decisions that minimize expense while preserving system responsiveness and reliability. Fortunately, GCP provides several mechanisms—both at the service and billing levels— to help you run intelligent agents efficiently and economically.

The first principle in cost-effective MCP deployments is **selecting the right compute services** for the job. For stateless MCP endpoints (e.g., tool handlers or prompt processors), **Cloud Run** is often the most cost-efficient option. It charges only for the actual compute time consumed per request, with billing measured in milliseconds. For lightweight MCP resource handlers that do not need full containers, **Cloud Functions** offer an even simpler deployment model, ideal for low-traffic or event-driven components. Meanwhile, **GKE Autopilot** can be used for more advanced orchestration if you need to run a suite of tightly-coupled MCP modules or agent services continuously.

Next, reduce cold-start overhead and excessive invocations by **tuning concurrency settings**. For Cloud Run, increasing the concurrency limit allows multiple requests to be processed on a single instance, amortizing startup costs across more invocations. If your agents invoke tools or retrieve external context in tight loops, this optimization can drastically reduce costs over time.

Caching also plays a central role. Implement **in-memory caching with Memorystore** or external data caching with **Cloud CDN** for public resources. This is particularly valuable when MCP resources fetch contextual data that doesn't change frequently—e.g., pricing data, static reports, or known reference documents. By caching these payloads, you can reduce repeated function executions and associated compute charges.

Another often overlooked area is **egress and API usage**. MCP agents may consume external APIs such as Google Maps, language models, or internal REST services. To limit egress cost and API quota usage, centralize outbound calls within shared tools or use batching strategies when querying multiple data points. Also, take advantage of **VPC connectors** to keep traffic internal when possible, avoiding unnecessary public network charges.

Monitoring is key to avoiding cost surprises. GCP's **Billing Reports** and **Budgets & Alerts** allow you to track MCP system spend in near real-time. You can set up granular budgets at the project or service level—say, to alert you if Cloud Run usage exceeds $20 this week, or if outbound networking crosses a preset threshold. Pair these with **Cloud Monitoring dashboards** that track resource usage metrics (like request count, execution time, and memory allocation), giving you visibility into where cost hotspots are forming.

Storage costs can also creep up silently. Ensure your logs in **Cloud Logging** are not retained indefinitely unless necessary. Set up **log exclusions** or custom **retention policies** to delete old or low-priority logs (such as routine health checks) after a fixed period, like 7 or 30 days.

For persistent storage, consider **Cloud Storage lifecycle rules**, which automatically transition older objects to cheaper storage classes like Nearline or Coldline. This is ideal for agent-generated outputs or archived prompt histories that must be retained but are rarely accessed.

Finally, optimize your development and staging environments. Use **preemptible VMs** or temporary Cloud Run revisions to handle load tests and debugging without long-term resource reservations. Disable unused services or scale down test environments during off-hours using Cloud Scheduler jobs that stop GKE clusters or reduce autoscaling limits.

In summary, a cost-effective GCP deployment for MCP agents blends service selection, concurrency tuning, caching, monitoring, and smart budgeting. By staying vigilant and proactively tuning both your architecture and your billing visibility, you ensure your intelligent agent systems scale economically—enabling more innovation per dollar spent.

Part V – Advanced Architecture and Future Directions

Chapter 14: Context Management Techniques

14.1 Using Vector DBs to Augment Agent Knowledge

Context is the heartbeat of intelligent agent behavior, and as AI systems become more complex, the ability to store, retrieve, and reason over contextual information at scale becomes a necessity—not a luxury. In the world of MCP-enabled agents, Vector Databases play a foundational role in giving agents memory-like capabilities and enhancing prompt accuracy through semantic retrieval. This section walks you through why vector databases are essential, how they fit into the MCP workflow, and how to implement them in a practical, production-ready pipeline.

At its core, a vector database allows you to store high-dimensional embeddings—numerical representations of text, images, or structured data—and efficiently search for semantically similar items. In the context of MCP, these embeddings might represent past user queries, long documents, code snippets, or prior agent-tool interactions. Instead of relying on keyword match or string comparison, agents retrieve relevant content by comparing vectors based on cosine similarity or other distance metrics.

Let's break it down with a real-world implementation using [official commentary from tools like] Pinecone or ChromaDB, both widely adopted for production-ready AI agents. Suppose your MCP agent is a legal assistant. When a user asks a question about "termination clauses in employment contracts," you don't want to return canned responses or unrelated information. Instead, the agent can embed the user's query using a pre-configured language model (e.g., OpenAI's `text-embedding-ada-002`) and use that vector to search a collection of previously indexed case law, policy documents, and HR handbooks stored in a vector DB.

Assuming you already have a set of PDFs or Markdown documents loaded as resources within your MCP tool, the first step is to split the content into manageable chunks (e.g., 500 tokens), embed each chunk, and insert it into the vector database along with metadata (source, date, tags). During query time, the MCP agent executes the following steps: it receives the user's prompt, generates the embedding of that prompt, queries the vector DB for top-N similar chunks, and injects the results back into the context window of the prompt being sent to the LLM. This is RAG—Retrieval-Augmented Generation—in practice, embedded directly into your MCP pipeline.

Here's a simplified illustration using Python with ChromaDB:

```python
from langchain.vectorstores import Chroma
from langchain.embeddings import OpenAIEmbeddings

# Initialize vector DB and embedding engine
embedding = OpenAIEmbeddings()
db = Chroma(persist_directory="./law_corpus",
embedding_function=embedding)

# Search the database
query = "What are termination rights for contractors in
Texas?"
results = db.similarity_search(query, k=3)

# Format for LLM prompt context
retrieved_context = "\n".join([doc.page_content for doc in
results])
```

This retrieved context can now be passed into the MCP prompt resource to ensure the agent has all relevant legal information injected in real time. By configuring this as an MCP resource, you can expose it to agents across your deployment stack without duplicating logic or embedding code in each prompt manually.

The benefits are numerous: reduced hallucination, improved response specificity, dynamic context updates without retraining the base model, and scalable memory without bloating the prompt window.

In closing, vector databases are not just an enhancement—they are a pillar of modern context-aware agent design. Whether used to simulate long-term memory, deliver focused document lookups, or dynamically adjust behavior across use cases, vector DBs unlock a new level of precision and intelligence in MCP-powered systems.

14.2 Memory Persistence for Long-Running Agents

As AI agents evolve from short-lived stateless services into long-running, autonomous processes, memory persistence becomes a non-negotiable requirement. Long-running agents—especially those operating within the Model Context Protocol (MCP) architecture—must maintain continuity across multiple interactions, workflows, and time windows. This continuity allows agents to learn from experience, recall past states, and exhibit behaviors that mimic reasoning over time. Without persistent memory, agents risk becoming brittle, repetitive, or disconnected from user context.

In MCP-based systems, memory persistence is the practice of storing agent state, context data, intermediate outputs, and decision history across sessions or timeframes. The challenge is not just about storing this data—but doing so in a structured, queryable, and secure manner that integrates smoothly with the MCP server and its JSON-RPC interface.

Let's consider a practical case. Imagine an MCP-powered customer support agent assisting users across multiple days or tickets. On day one, the user inquires about a payment failure. On day three, they return with a related complaint. Without memory, the agent would treat these as two isolated events. But with persistent memory, the agent can recall the customer's last session, summarize prior interactions, and proactively continue the resolution process.

Implementing this typically involves integrating a persistence layer—such as a database or document store—that saves structured memory objects associated with the user session or agent thread. These objects can include:

- A running dialogue history
- Tool usage logs and results
- Relevant embeddings or semantic tags
- Named entities and extracted user preferences
- Task status (e.g., "payment issue unresolved")

Within MCP, these memory structures are exposed via **Resources**, allowing both agents and tools to query or update memory state seamlessly.

Let's walk through a simplified example using SQLite for persistent memory. First, define a schema for storing session data:

```
CREATE TABLE session_memory (
    session_id TEXT PRIMARY KEY,
    user_name TEXT,
    conversation_history TEXT,
    last_updated TIMESTAMP DEFAULT CURRENT_TIMESTAMP
```

```
);
```

Now in Python, your MCP resource function might look like this:

```
def get_memory(session_id):
    cursor = db.cursor()
    cursor.execute("SELECT conversation_history FROM
session_memory WHERE session_id = ?", (session_id,))
    result = cursor.fetchone()
    return result[0] if result else ""

def update_memory(session_id, new_entry):
    existing = get_memory(session_id)
    updated_history = existing + "\n" + new_entry
    db.execute(
        "INSERT OR REPLACE INTO session_memory (session_id,
conversation_history) VALUES (?, ?)",
        (session_id, updated_history)
    )
    db.commit()
```

This can be wired into your MCP server as a resource that tools or prompt generators can call before responding. The key is to maintain this separation of concerns—tools generate or consume information, while the memory layer quietly ensures continuity and coherence across steps.

Depending on your architecture, you may use PostgreSQL, MongoDB, Redis, or even cloud-native storage (e.g., AWS DynamoDB or Firestore) to persist memory across distributed services. You can also integrate vector embeddings into your memory model for similarity-based recall (combining 14.1 and 14.2).

Critically, memory updates must be versioned and timestamped. This prevents overwrites, supports auditing, and enables features like "rollback" or "memory pruning." In production environments, also consider encryption, access control, and memory lifespan policies.

In summary, memory persistence empowers MCP agents with temporal awareness. It turns agents from reactive chatbots into proactive collaborators, capable of maintaining continuity across interactions. By architecting a robust memory layer—tightly coupled with MCP resources—you unlock a new dimension of intelligence, reliability, and user trust in your agent systems.

14.3 Filtering Context Dynamically for Prompt Limits

As large language models continue to evolve, the amount of contextual information they can handle in a single prompt remains constrained by token limits. This poses a unique challenge for developers working with the Model Context Protocol (MCP), especially when designing agents that interact with vast, evolving memory or external knowledge sources. Dynamic context filtering becomes essential—not just for technical feasibility, but for performance, latency, and cost optimization.

Context filtering in MCP refers to the selective curation of relevant information before injecting it into a prompt. Since agents often maintain long-running conversations, fetch resource-heavy data, or access semantic memory, the total token count can easily exceed the model's input window. Without a filtering mechanism, agents either fail, truncate critical data, or degrade in quality due to loss of precision.

The solution lies in building a dynamic context pre-processor that ranks, scores, or prunes the available data before it enters the prompt template. This pre-processing can happen either in the client application (before an `mcp.invoke()` call) or server-side (as a resource or tool filter). MCP's modular architecture makes this pattern easy to implement.

Let's walk through a practical implementation pattern. Suppose your agent has access to a rich memory resource—a structured object storing chat history, named entities, external database lookups, and previous tool outputs. Instead of dumping this entire state into the prompt, you score and extract only what's most relevant to the current query.

Here's a simplified example in Python that illustrates this process:

```
def filter_context(current_query, memory_chunks,
token_limit):
    # memory_chunks: list of (chunk, score) tuples
    scored_chunks = []

    for chunk in memory_chunks:
        # Score relevance based on simple keyword overlap or
embedding similarity
```

```
        score = relevance_score(current_query, chunk)
        scored_chunks.append((chunk, score))

    # Sort chunks by descending score
    scored_chunks.sort(key=lambda x: x[1], reverse=True)

    # Iteratively add chunks until token limit is reached
    selected_chunks = []
    total_tokens = 0

    for chunk, _ in scored_chunks:
        chunk_tokens = count_tokens(chunk)
        if total_tokens + chunk_tokens <= token_limit:
            selected_chunks.append(chunk)
            total_tokens += chunk_tokens
        else:
            break

    return selected_chunks
```

In practice, `relevance_score()` might be implemented using cosine similarity between embeddings (e.g., via OpenAI's `text-embedding-3-small` or SentenceTransformers), while `count_tokens()` estimates token usage via a tokenizer like `tiktoken`.

You can expose this logic as a dedicated MCP tool called `context.filter`, or bake it directly into your MCP prompt generation logic. The result is a prompt like the following:

```
prompt = f"""
You are an assistant helping with project planning.
Use only the following context:
{filtered_context}
User's latest question: {user_query}
"""
```

This approach scales well in environments where token budgets are tight, model latency must be minimized, or context is composed from diverse sources (chat history, vector store hits, recent events, etc.).

Dynamic context filtering also plays a critical role in compliance. By controlling what enters the prompt, you can avoid leaking sensitive information, enforce tenant isolation, or implement data expiration logic.

These concerns become paramount in multi-user, production-grade agents deployed through MCP.

In closing, context filtering is more than just a workaround for token limits. It's a powerful design pattern that lets MCP agents remain precise, performant, and secure—regardless of the complexity or volume of their memory and data streams. When built correctly, it ensures every prompt is focused, relevant, and within budget—without compromising on capability.

14.4 Streaming Data and Large Context Chunking

In scenarios where AI agents must process vast or continuous streams of data—such as logs, event feeds, documents, or real-time user activity—the challenge isn't just storage, but how to selectively feed this data into large language models (LLMs) via prompt windows that have strict token limits. Within the Model Context Protocol (MCP), this situation calls for a strategy known as *context chunking*—breaking up large data into meaningful, query-relevant segments—and optionally *streaming* them as needed.

MCP provides a modular structure where tools and resources can act as data brokers. These modules can retrieve, stream, or chunk content dynamically before that content is formatted into the prompt. This architecture allows MCP agents to interface with systems such as Kafka, S3, Firehose, SQL databases, or blob storage and progressively inject useful context in manageable units.

To understand how this works in practice, consider a real-world use case where an agent must summarize a lengthy PDF report stored in cloud storage. Loading the entire document into a single prompt will quickly exceed the input limit of most foundation models. The approach, then, is to preprocess the document server-side into semantically coherent chunks—like paragraphs or sections—then serve them incrementally to the LLM based on relevance or a sliding window.

Here's a basic illustration of chunking and streaming within an MCP resource:

```
# Simplified chunking logic for large text
def chunk_text(text, max_tokens_per_chunk):
    import tiktoken
    tokenizer = tiktoken.encoding_for_model("gpt-4")
```

```
    words = text.split()
    chunks = []
    current_chunk = []

    for word in words:
        current_chunk.append(word)
        token_count = len(tokenizer.encode("
".join(current_chunk)))
        if token_count > max_tokens_per_chunk:
            # Remove last word that overflowed
            current_chunk.pop()
            chunks.append(" ".join(current_chunk))
            current_chunk = [word]   # Start next chunk

    if current_chunk:
        chunks.append(" ".join(current_chunk))

    return chunks
```

Once the chunks are generated, the MCP resource can stream them based on a `cursor` or `offset` value sent from the client. For example, the client might call the resource like so:

```
{
  "jsonrpc": "2.0",
  "method": "resource.get_chunk",
  "params": {
    "document_id": "annual-report-2024",
    "chunk_index": 3
  },
  "id": "42"
}
```

Each invocation returns the next relevant chunk, which the client or orchestrator can inject into the prompt pipeline. This model also supports live or tailing data. For example, in a DevOps monitoring scenario, an MCP tool could be wired to stream logs from a container and chunk them into short bursts, with each chunk being evaluated for anomalies or patterns by an LLM.

MCP also makes this even more flexible by allowing agents to *react to each chunk*. For example, agents can process a chunk, produce an intermediate summary or signal, and then decide whether to request the next chunk or stop—enabling agentic flow control.

Furthermore, when dealing with truly massive datasets, chunking can be paired with retrieval-based filtering. You might first embed all chunks and store them in a vector database, then perform similarity search before selecting a subset for prompt construction. This strategy avoids brute-force streaming and prioritizes relevance.

In closing, large context chunking and streaming are vital patterns for building intelligent, scalable agents with MCP. They enable structured access to unbounded or high-volume data sources while ensuring that prompt payloads remain within model constraints. By combining chunking with semantic filtering, cursor-based access, and iterative prompting, MCP developers can create agents that digest extensive data sets intelligently and progressively—without overwhelming the system or losing control over inference budgets.

14.5 Future of Context: Multi-Modal, Cross-Agent, External Memory

As language models evolve beyond text-only capabilities, the concept of "context" is rapidly expanding to include multimodal signals, shared memory across agents, and persistent context accessible through external storage. In the Model Context Protocol (MCP), context has always been a first-class citizen—but to build next-generation agents that are adaptable, collaborative, and perceptive, developers must rethink context as a dynamic, extensible, and shared asset.

The future of context begins with **multi-modal support**. Agents are no longer limited to consuming strings of text. Vision-capable models like GPT-4o, Gemini, and Claude can process images, audio, and even video. Within MCP, this requires resource modules that can preprocess non-text inputs—extracting features, converting them into embeddings, or generating intermediate text descriptions. For example, an MCP resource might accept a base64-encoded image, send it to a model for captioning, and inject the description into the prompt:

```
{
  "jsonrpc": "2.0",
  "method": "resource.describe_image",
```

```
    "params": {
        "image_blob": "<base64-encoded-jpeg>"
    },
    "id": "img01"
}
```

This output can be used as prompt context for a diagnostic agent, QA system, or a visual assistant. Future-ready MCP agents should treat vision and audio resources just like textual tools—invokable, composable, and streamed when needed.

In parallel, we are moving toward **cross-agent context sharing**. Imagine a set of agents working on subtasks—one focused on user intent classification, another on document search, and a third on summarization. Rather than each agent retrieving and duplicating context, they can use a **shared context pool**, either memory-based or database-backed, accessible via MCP APIs. This allows one agent to write to the context space and others to read from it— enabling coordination without reprocessing.

Here's an example of how an agent might contribute to shared memory:

```
{
    "jsonrpc": "2.0",
    "method": "context.write",
    "params": {
        "key": "session:user123:last_prompt",
        "value": "Summarize the Q2 performance review"
    },
    "id": "ctx-01"
}
```

Other agents can then retrieve this value during their reasoning cycle using `context.read`. This supports *distributed cognition*—a vital ingredient for agentic systems where multiple models act collaboratively in real time.

Another emerging direction is **external memory systems**. These aren't just caches or databases—they are architected as long-term, structured memories that agents can query, update, and reason over. They store user preferences, session history, task results, and long-term state. Technologies such as Redis, Pinecone, Weaviate, or even file-based embeddings can serve this role, often wrapped behind MCP tools or resources. The goal is to decouple memory from the model, making agents stateless but context-rich.

Consider an agent that offloads its internal state to a vector store:

```json
{
  "jsonrpc": "2.0",
  "method": "memory.upsert_vector",
  "params": {
    "namespace": "project_briefings",
    "id": "briefing_2024_q1",
    "embedding": [...],
    "metadata": {
      "title": "Q1 Strategy Update",
      "tags": ["briefing", "2024"]
    }
  },
  "id": "m01"
}
```

Later, an agent can search this store to rehydrate context relevant to a user's query or a task in progress.

To support these new modalities and memory patterns, MCP itself will need to grow: adopting standardized MIME types, chunked streaming payloads, persistent handles to memory, and authentication across agents and services. These changes will transform MCP into a robust substrate for **multimodal, memory-augmented, cross-agent communication**.

In summary, the future of context lies in making it richer (multi-modal), smarter (memory-aware), and more collaborative (cross-agent). Developers who embrace these paradigms with MCP will unlock powerful capabilities— from agents that remember long-term goals and see what users see, to networks of AI collaborators exchanging insights in real time. Context will no longer be a static input—it will be the living substrate of intelligent behavior.

Chapter 15: Architecture Patterns for MCP-Based AI Agents

15.1 Single-Agent vs. Multi-Agent Use Cases

When designing AI agents with the Model Context Protocol (MCP), a foundational decision lies in choosing between a single-agent or multi-agent architecture. This choice impacts system complexity, scalability, fault tolerance, performance, and the types of problems your solution can effectively solve. MCP is flexible enough to support both paradigms, but each comes with trade-offs that must be carefully considered depending on your application's goals.

A **single-agent architecture** typically involves one core AI agent interacting with the environment or user, supported by MCP tools and resources. This is ideal for linear or bounded tasks like summarization, code generation, or Q&A where context is well-scoped and the task can be completed with minimal coordination. The agent sends prompts enriched with MCP resources (e.g., document fetchers, database queries) and invokes tools to act on decisions it makes. The communication loop is relatively simple: the client submits a prompt, the agent processes it with available context, and the system returns a result.

Here's an example JSON-RPC invocation pattern from a single-agent setup:

```
{
  "jsonrpc": "2.0",
  "method": "tool.generate_sql",
  "params": {
    "natural_language_query": "Get top 5 customers by revenue
in 2024"
  },
  "id": "t01"
}
```

This call may be followed by a second one to execute the query or format the results, but the agent remains the single locus of control.

In contrast, **multi-agent architectures** involve several specialized agents collaborating to achieve a shared objective. MCP's decoupled design shines here: each agent may be its own client, operating with a different context scope, and using shared tools or resources. Agents can invoke each other's services, exchange intermediate outputs via MCP's memory APIs, and delegate subtasks dynamically. This is especially powerful in complex workflows like document analysis, multi-turn planning, autonomous research, or code refactoring where modular, domain-specific reasoning is critical.

Imagine a scenario where three agents operate concurrently:

- A **Retriever Agent** fetches relevant documents via an MCP resource.
- A **Summarizer Agent** extracts key insights.
- A **Planner Agent** creates follow-up tasks based on those insights.

Each agent works independently but shares access to memory and logging services. Communication flows via context handles or chain-of-prompt outputs. A typical exchange may look like this:

```
{
  "jsonrpc": "2.0",
  "method": "context.write",
  "params": {
    "key": "retriever/latest_docs",
    "value": [ "doc_23", "doc_24", "doc_25" ]
  },
  "id": "ctx01"
}
```

Another agent may read this context to inform its own processing:

```
{
  "jsonrpc": "2.0",
  "method": "context.read",
  "params": {
    "key": "retriever/latest_docs"
  },
  "id": "ctx02"
}
```

This decoupled, modular pattern enables greater reuse and testability. For example, individual agents can be hot-swapped, versioned, or deployed independently. Error handling becomes more granular, and failures in one agent don't necessarily compromise the whole system.

However, multi-agent systems require additional orchestration and logging discipline. Developers must design shared context boundaries, implement robust observability (e.g., which agent triggered what tool), and ensure that agents can gracefully handle missing or stale data from peer contexts. Techniques such as retries, fallback agents, and quorum-based voting become valuable in distributed decision-making.

In summary, single-agent MCP designs are fast to implement and easy to manage, best suited for atomic tasks or bounded domains. Multi-agent systems, on the other hand, embrace modularity and collaboration, enabling sophisticated, layered problem solving. MCP provides the primitives to support both—from isolated RPC flows to shared memory, concurrent prompts, and inter-agent context management. The key is to map your problem domain to the right architectural model, start with minimal viable orchestration, and grow complexity only when necessary.

15.2 Modularization vs. Monolithic Architectures

When building AI agents with the Model Context Protocol (MCP), one of the most consequential architectural decisions is whether to pursue a **monolithic design**—where all logic, tools, and context handling live within a single tightly integrated application—or a **modularized architecture**—where components are distributed across isolated, reusable units like separate services, tool servers, and context providers. MCP encourages modularity by design, but understanding the trade-offs of both patterns is critical for production-grade systems.

A **monolithic architecture** groups all functionalities—agent logic, prompt templating, tools, resources, memory interactions—into a unified deployment unit. This approach is straightforward for prototyping and small-scale use cases. It enables faster iteration since everything is accessible in one place, with minimal overhead for inter-process communication or service discovery. For instance, an agent that summarizes meeting transcripts, books appointments, and sends follow-ups may encapsulate all tool implementations and context processing within a single server running behind one MCP endpoint.

Let's consider a simplified monolithic MCP server setup. All tool methods are defined in one Python file:

```
@tool("summarize_text")
def summarize_text(context: ToolCallContext, input_text: str)
-> str:
    return some_summarizer(input_text)

@tool("schedule_meeting")
def schedule_meeting(context: ToolCallContext, datetime: str)
-> str:
    return calendar_api.schedule(datetime)
```

This design is efficient and sufficient for bounded tasks. However, as complexity grows—especially with multi-agent systems, third-party data integrations, and independent scaling requirements—monolithic structures quickly become brittle. Code becomes tightly coupled, error boundaries are hard to isolate, and deployments become riskier.

On the other hand, **modular architectures** decompose the system into independently deployed, logically separated units. MCP facilitates this through its JSON-RPC message model, allowing clients to call any tool or resource hosted across servers as long as they adhere to the protocol. You can register tools on separate endpoints, delegate context management to specialized services, and isolate prompt templates from logic execution.

Here's an example of modular architecture in practice:

- A **Tool Server** exposes data transformation and summarization tools.
- A **Resource Server** fetches information from APIs or databases and returns contextual fragments.
- A **Memory Server** handles persistent conversation history or external vector store access.
- The main **Agent Server** orchestrates the overall prompt logic and response flow.

Each component can be updated, monitored, and scaled independently. Suppose your summarization load spikes but not your calendar booking. You can scale the summarizer's container separately without impacting the rest of the system. Moreover, versioning and testing become more manageable: you can A/B test a new summarizer tool without changing the rest of the stack.

For example, the summarization tool can live in its own dedicated microservice:

```
{
  "jsonrpc": "2.0",
  "method": "summarizer.summarize",
  "params": {
    "text": "meeting notes content..."
  },
  "id": "tool_1"
}
```

This tool could be hosted on its own MCP-compliant server and registered dynamically by the agent. It allows for language-specific optimizations (e.g., Python for NLP tools, Go for fast context fetchers) and easier integration of third-party APIs with secure tokens or rate limits.

Still, modularization introduces orchestration overhead. You need robust service discovery, retry logic, standardized interfaces, and error isolation. This is where shared memory (via `context.read` and `context.write`) and logging hooks help coordinate behavior across components.

In Summary, monolithic designs are simpler and faster for small projects, but scale poorly and resist flexibility. Modular MCP architectures, though initially more complex, unlock scalable, maintainable, and interoperable systems. The best practice is to **start monolithic** for clarity, **identify modular seams** (e.g., tools that can live independently), and **gradually extract services** as workloads increase. With MCP's decoupled RPC architecture, you're already future-proofing your agent system by building on a modular-ready foundation.

15.3 Adding Human Oversight with Review/Approval Flows

As AI agents grow more autonomous and are trusted with high-impact decisions—whether generating content, initiating transactions, or automating workflows—integrating **human oversight** becomes not just a safety mechanism but a critical design principle. The Model Context Protocol (MCP), by virtue of its decoupled, transparent invocation model, provides a natural way to embed review and approval checkpoints within an agent's workflow without breaking its autonomy loop.

156

In MCP-enabled systems, every tool or resource call is a discrete, trackable JSON-RPC method. This allows developers to intercept specific actions for human validation before they are executed or propagated. For instance, when an agent attempts to submit a report, approve an invoice, or respond to a high-stakes customer query, the tool invocation can be redirected to a **review middleware**—a registered MCP tool responsible for queuing the request, notifying a human reviewer, and awaiting their decision.

Here's how this would work in practice. Let's say the agent invokes a function like `submit_final_report`. Instead of letting this execute immediately, you route it through a human approval tool:

```json
{
  "jsonrpc": "2.0",
  "method": "review_queue.request_approval",
  "params": {
    "action": "submit_final_report",
    "payload": {
      "report_content": "Full financial summary attached."
    },
    "initiated_by": "agent_42",
    "urgency": "high"
  },
  "id": "review_1"
}
```

The `review_queue.request_approval` tool implementation would log the request, generate a review link (perhaps via a web dashboard), notify the assigned approver (via Slack, email, or a portal), and hold execution until the approver gives explicit go-ahead. Once the human response is received (either "approve" or "reject"), the system either continues execution or halts with a reason.

From the agent's perspective, it receives the approval decision as a normal response:

```json
{
  "jsonrpc": "2.0",
  "result": {
    "status": "approved",
    "reviewer": "manager_joe"
  },
  "id": "review_1"
```

157

```
}
```

If approved, the agent can proceed to call the actual `submit_final_report` tool. If rejected, it can escalate, rephrase, or stop.

This oversight pattern supports many real-world needs:

- **Legal or compliance sign-off** before filing sensitive documents.
- **Human moderation** of AI-generated content before publishing.
- **Supervisor checks** on high-cost decisions like budget allocations.
- **Customer support escalation** for emotional or ambiguous cases.

By decoupling human interaction from agent logic through an MCP-wrapped tool, you preserve the benefits of automation while still meeting accountability, trust, and ethical requirements. The human-in-the-loop step doesn't require the agent to "understand" human decisions—it just needs to query a tool and respond based on output, like any other API call.

It's also possible to log and audit all approval requests via MCP's logging hooks, ensuring traceability and supporting compliance audits.

In summary, MCP's modular invocation pattern makes it straightforward to plug human reviewers into the execution path of autonomous agents. This empowers developers to balance automation speed with human judgment and create safer, more trustworthy systems. Whether applied to internal approvals, customer interaction, or regulatory processes, review flows with MCP become a seamless extension of the agent workflow—enabling **accountable AI** at scale.

15.4 Blending LLM Agents with Legacy Services

Integrating large language model (LLM) agents into enterprise environments often requires them to interface with legacy systems—those older yet mission-critical services that may lack modern APIs, have rigid schemas, or depend on outdated protocols. The Model Context Protocol (MCP) excels in this environment by acting as a bridge between next-generation AI agents and these entrenched systems, enabling seamless interaction without requiring legacy code rewrites or complex API transformations.

At its core, MCP provides a standardized, JSON-RPC-based interface that abstracts the internal mechanics of any tool or resource. This makes it ideal for wrapping legacy services—whether they run on SOAP, command-line scripts, relational databases, or message queues—behind a clean, stateless function call. The agent doesn't need to understand how the system works; it only needs to call the MCP-registered tool and handle the result.

For example, suppose your organization relies on a legacy HR system that only exposes a SOAP interface to retrieve employee records. Rather than attempting to embed SOAP logic directly into the LLM agent or LangChain flow, you can create a dedicated MCP tool like `hr_legacy.get_employee_info` that encapsulates the SOAP interaction internally. Here's how an agent might invoke it:

```
{
  "jsonrpc": "2.0",
  "method": "hr_legacy.get_employee_info",
  "params": {
    "employee_id": "EMP-98345"
  },
  "id": "call_1"
}
```

Behind the scenes, this MCP tool calls a Python or Node.js wrapper that converts the JSON payload to a SOAP request, parses the XML response, and transforms it into structured JSON. The agent receives a clean, language-model-friendly output:

```
{
  "jsonrpc": "2.0",
  "result": {
    "name": "Dana Richards",
    "position": "Senior Engineer",
    "last_promotion_date": "2022-04-01"
  },
  "id": "call_1"
}
```

This abstraction empowers the LLM to reason over legacy data and incorporate it into tasks such as generating reports, onboarding new hires, or flagging overdue promotions—all without ever knowing the complexities of the underlying HR platform.

This same approach works for:

- Mainframe systems accessed via CLI or Telnet
- SQL databases with limited or no modern ORM support
- FTP-based document stores
- Email-based workflows requiring parsing of legacy formats

Additionally, the MCP host can enforce retry logic, circuit breakers, or fallback responses when legacy services are slow or unreliable. You can even log all legacy service calls centrally through MCP's built-in observability hooks, enabling better debugging, auditing, and optimization over time.

By wrapping legacy services in well-defined, stateless MCP tools, you decouple the agent's reasoning layer from fragile or non-standard backend systems. This not only improves maintainability and testability, but also future-proofs your infrastructure, allowing you to replace or upgrade legacy systems gradually without disrupting agent workflows.

In summary, MCP's power lies in its ability to act as a translation layer between modern LLM agents and legacy enterprise systems. This enables organizations to deploy intelligent agents today—without waiting for every backend to modernize—by embracing interoperability, encapsulation, and clean abstraction through MCP tools.

15.5 Designing Maintainable, Scalable Agent Architectures with MCP

As AI agents transition from proof-of-concept demos to critical components in enterprise infrastructure, scalability and maintainability become essential. The Model Context Protocol (MCP) is uniquely positioned to support these needs by offering a standardized, modular, and interoperable interface for building distributed agent systems. In this section, we focus on how to architect MCP-based systems that scale efficiently while remaining easy to maintain over time.

A maintainable architecture begins with **separation of concerns**. MCP enables this by allowing developers to encapsulate logic into distinct tools and resources. Each MCP tool can focus on a single responsibility—such as retrieving a user profile, triggering an automation workflow, or summarizing a document—without being tightly coupled to the agent's reasoning engine. This makes the system easy to test, debug, and update independently.

Similarly, MCP resources serve as clear interfaces for context provisioning, such as real-time metrics, knowledge bases, or user session state.

To support scalability, MCP decouples agents from backend service logic. Rather than embedding logic directly into the agent, an agent simply issues JSON-RPC calls to registered tools. These tools can be executed in isolated environments, scaled horizontally, or offloaded to specialized microservices. This clean separation allows infrastructure teams to scale individual components—such as rate-limited APIs or heavy computation workloads—without needing to modify agent behavior.

Consider an enterprise system serving multiple product teams. Each team can define their own set of MCP tools that expose internal systems. These tools can then be registered into a central MCP server or multiple tenant-isolated servers. A shared client agent (such as a support bot or documentation assistant) can dynamically choose tools based on availability, tenant context, or workload policies—making the system modular and resilient.

For example, a scalable agent architecture might look like this:

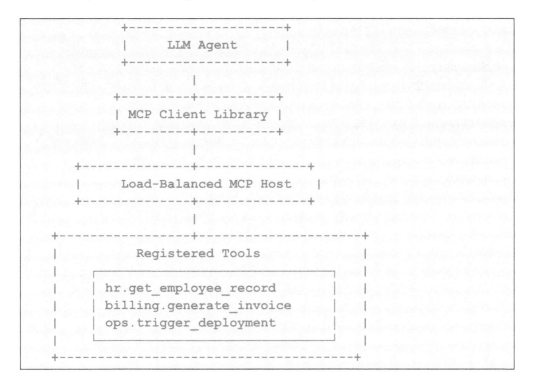

Each of the tool handlers above can live in separate containers or services and be scaled based on usage metrics. You can configure caching layers, queue-based job execution, or fallback strategies to ensure the system remains performant under load.

From a maintainability standpoint, MCP encourages:

- **Stateless functions**: Tools and resources should not maintain internal state, reducing complexity.
- **Explicit versioning**: Methods like `customer.get_profile_v2` allow for backward compatibility.
- **Schema definition and validation**: Using JSON schemas or similar techniques ensures agents only send and receive valid data.
- **Logging and observability**: MCP's JSON-RPC format can be extended with structured logs, making it easy to audit and trace tool invocations.

As the system grows, teams can introduce **tool discovery and registration protocols**, allowing new services to self-register with MCP hosts. Combined with permission enforcement, tenancy-aware routing, and environment configuration management, this unlocks automated deployment pipelines and production-grade observability.

In Summary, MCP provides a clean foundation for designing agent architectures that are easy to reason about, test, scale, and evolve. Its design promotes modularity, enables isolated development, and supports robust communication patterns. By building on these principles, developers can create agentic systems that not only meet today's needs but also grow with organizational demands—without collapsing under the weight of complexity.

Chapter 16: Agent Orchestration and Coordination

16.1 Designing Sequential Task Chains

As AI agents grow more capable, their tasks often extend beyond single-step completions into coordinated, multi-step operations. Sequential task chaining is one of the simplest and most powerful orchestration patterns available to developers working with the Model Context Protocol (MCP). It allows developers to break complex goals into discrete, ordered tasks executed one after the other—where each task's output may inform or drive the next. This approach creates predictable workflows and is especially well-suited for use cases like document pipelines, report generation, staged data enrichment, and multi-stage decision-making.

MCP's architecture makes sequential chaining intuitive. Each tool exposed through the MCP server is a callable JSON-RPC method, and agents using MCP clients can call these methods one at a time, await their output, and pass results into the next call in the sequence. This aligns perfectly with prompt-based control structures or orchestrated flows in autonomous agents.

Let's walk through a real-world example to illustrate the flow. Imagine you are building an AI research assistant that automates the following sequence: (1) fetch a research article, (2) summarize the abstract, (3) generate follow-up questions based on the summary, and (4) propose relevant citations using an external vector search. Each of these steps can be represented by a distinct MCP tool.

Here's how this might look in a Python agent using the MCP client:

```python
from mcp_client import import MCPClient

client = MCPClient(server_url="http://localhost:8000")

# Step 1: Fetch article
article = client.call("research.fetch_paper", {"doi":
"10.1000/xyz123"})

# Step 2: Summarize abstract
summary = client.call("nlp.summarize_text", {"text":
article["abstract"]})
```

```
# Step 3: Generate questions
questions = client.call("nlp.generate_questions",
{"input_text": summary})

# Step 4: Retrieve similar papers
citations = client.call("knowledge.vector_search", {"query":
summary})
```

In this example, each step depends on the output of the previous one. The agent doesn't make assumptions—it pauses and waits for valid, complete responses before proceeding. This model provides transparency, simplicity, and easy debugging: if a failure occurs at any point, it's clear which tool caused it, and the sequence can be retried or halted accordingly.

To support robust chaining in production systems, developers should implement consistent output formats, versioning of methods, and fallback strategies (e.g., skip or retry on tool failure). Additionally, by storing intermediate results in structured memory or a temporary context object, agents can reuse outputs or audit decisions at each stage.

This chaining logic can also be implemented within prompt templates using in-context learning. For example, you might prompt a language model with the summary and then embed instructions like: "Based on the above, generate 5 exploratory research questions." This approach leverages both MCP-based tooling and LLM prompt reasoning, giving agents hybrid control over logic and language.

In summary, sequential task chains allow agents to execute structured workflows in a transparent, maintainable, and modular way. By exposing atomic functions through MCP tools and combining them in code, developers can turn linear reasoning paths into powerful, repeatable behaviors. This design forms the foundation for more complex orchestration strategies like branching logic, retries, and even conditional or looped executions covered in later sections.

16.2 Parallel Agents and Role-Based Interactions

As AI systems evolve to tackle increasingly complex and time-sensitive problems, the need for concurrency and specialization within agent workflows becomes critical. While sequential task chaining offers predictability, it often limits throughput and responsiveness. Parallel agent execution—where multiple agents operate simultaneously, each fulfilling a distinct role—enables scalable, high-performance systems capable of intelligent multitasking. The Model Context Protocol (MCP) provides a natural framework to support such architectures by decoupling tools, resources, and context-aware tasks across distributed actors.

At the core of this model is the idea of **role-based interactions**. Each agent in a parallel workflow is designed with a specific responsibility, such as data enrichment, validation, summarization, or decision-making. These roles are often mapped to specialized MCP tools or resource interfaces, allowing each agent to perform its task without bottlenecking others. This approach mirrors how microservices work in cloud architecture—isolated units, loosely coupled, communicating through defined protocols.

Let's consider a practical example. Suppose we're building a content analysis pipeline where an incoming article must be: (1) sentiment analyzed, (2) fact-checked, (3) summarized, and (4) assigned metadata for search indexing. Rather than executing these steps one after another, we can assign each task to a dedicated agent running in parallel. Each of these agents can connect to an MCP server and invoke the relevant tool independently.

Here's a conceptual structure in Python using `asyncio` to simulate parallel execution with MCP:

```python
import asyncio
from mcp_client import MCPClient

client = MCPClient("http://localhost:8000")

async def analyze_sentiment(article):
    return await client.acall("nlp.analyze_sentiment",
{"text": article})

async def fact_check(article):
    return await client.acall("nlp.fact_check", {"text":
article})

async def summarize(article):
    return await client.acall("nlp.summarize_text", {"text":
article})

async def extract_metadata(article):
```

```
    return await client.acall("meta.extract", {"text":
article})

async def run_parallel_analysis(article):
    results = await asyncio.gather(
        analyze_sentiment(article),
        fact_check(article),
        summarize(article),
        extract_metadata(article)
    )
    return {
        "sentiment": results[0],
        "fact_check": results[1],
        "summary": results[2],
        "metadata": results[3]
    }

# Sample run
article_text = "Recent studies have shown a rapid increase in
AI adoption across industries..."
results = asyncio.run(run_parallel_analysis(article_text))
```

Each function here maps directly to an MCP tool. Importantly, all tasks begin concurrently and complete as soon as their respective MCP endpoints return responses. This means the full analysis completes in the time of the slowest sub-task, not the total time of all steps combined. In a real deployment, each of these could be handled by distinct containerized agents pulling jobs from a queue or responding to streaming inputs.

From a systems design perspective, role-based parallelism encourages better modularity and testability. Each agent can be developed, deployed, and scaled independently. For example, if summarization is CPU-intensive, it can be allocated more resources or replicated without affecting the others. This also aligns well with orchestrators like Ray, Prefect, or serverless compute models like AWS Lambda and Azure Functions.

Furthermore, because MCP standardizes communication via JSON-RPC, these agents don't need to share the same language, runtime, or even infrastructure layer. A Node.js agent can perform fact-checking while a Python agent handles summarization—all as long as they speak MCP.

To ensure data consistency and reliability in these parallel workflows, developers must establish shared context management (e.g., using Redis, shared file systems, or vector databases) and carefully handle exceptions. If one agent fails, the orchestration layer should be able to retry, fallback, or exclude that output based on business rules.

In Summary, parallel agents and role-based interactions enable MCP-based systems to perform faster, scale horizontally, and operate with higher specialization. By structuring agents to align with clearly defined roles and leveraging concurrency, developers can architect AI workflows that are both efficient and resilient—key traits for real-world deployment at scale.

16.3 Orchestration Tools: Semantic Kernel and Beyond

As AI applications scale in complexity, the coordination of multiple agents, tools, and tasks becomes a significant challenge. While MCP provides a standardized protocol for enabling context-aware interactions between agents and components, orchestrating *how* and *when* these agents interact—especially in workflows with branching logic, memory handling, retries, and real-time decisions—requires a higher-level orchestration layer. Tools like Microsoft's **Semantic Kernel (SK)**, LangGraph, and Prefect have emerged to address these coordination challenges by offering programmable agentic workflows, memory integration, and modular planning capabilities.

Semantic Kernel is an open-source orchestration framework that abstracts prompt engineering, function invocation, and agent memory into a cohesive pipeline. It is designed to integrate traditional code and AI-native capabilities in the same application, using a planner and skill-based architecture. When used in combination with MCP, SK can act as a conductor—issuing JSON-RPC calls to MCP servers while reasoning about context, state, and output in the orchestration logic itself.

Let's examine how this works in practice. Suppose we want to build a document processing agent that performs the following: extract structured fields, summarize content, and validate facts. Each step is served by a different MCP tool exposed by an MCP server. Here's a conceptual flow using Semantic Kernel with Python:

```python
from semantic_kernel.kernel import Kernel
from semantic_kernel.orchestration.context import
ContextVariables
from semantic_kernel.connectors.ai.open_ai import
OpenAIChatCompletion
from mcp_client import MCPClient
```

```
kernel = Kernel()
kernel.add_text_completion_service("openai",
OpenAIChatCompletion("gpt-4", api_key="..."))

# Register custom MCP skill functions
mcp = MCPClient("http://localhost:8000")

async def extract_fields(input_text):
    return await mcp.acall("doc.extract_fields", {"text":
input_text})

async def summarize_text(input_text):
    return await mcp.acall("doc.summarize", {"text":
input_text})

async def validate_facts(input_text):
    return await mcp.acall("doc.fact_check", {"text":
input_text})

# Define planner-like workflow
async def run_workflow(input_text):
    context = ContextVariables(input_text)
    fields = await extract_fields(context.input)
    summary = await summarize_text(context.input)
    validation = await validate_facts(context.input)
    return {
        "fields": fields,
        "summary": summary,
        "validation": validation
    }
```

Although SK has its own internal planner for generating plans via LLMs, you can still call external MCP-based tools as part of any semantic function. This allows you to combine declarative planning with imperative RPC-based execution. More advanced use cases include chaining memory updates, parallel calls to tools, retry logic, and response re-ranking—all coordinated within SK but fulfilled via MCP services.

Beyond Semantic Kernel, tools like **LangGraph** and **CrewAI** offer specialized orchestration patterns for graph-based and multi-agent architectures. LangGraph allows developers to define nodes (representing agents or decision points) and edges (representing transitions), building complex workflows like state machines or reactive plans. MCP tools and resources can be injected into LangGraph nodes just like any function, giving you the ability to invoke external skills while preserving the standard JSON-RPC model.

Here's a minimal conceptual representation of a LangGraph with MCP integration:

```
from langgraph.graph import StateGraph
from mcp_client import MCPClient

mcp = MCPClient("http://localhost:8000")

async def node_extract(state):
    doc = state["document"]
    result = await mcp.acall("doc.extract_fields", {"text":
doc})
    return {"fields": result}

async def node_summarize(state):
    doc = state["document"]
    result = await mcp.acall("doc.summarize", {"text": doc})
    return {"summary": result}

builder = StateGraph()
builder.add_node("extract", node_extract)
builder.add_node("summarize", node_summarize)
builder.set_entry_point("extract")
builder.add_edge("extract", "summarize")

workflow = builder.compile()
result = await workflow.invoke({"document": "Full article
text here..."})
```

This orchestration model allows each node to represent one part of a larger, possibly branching, context-aware system. You can even combine event triggers, streaming updates, and conditional flows to build robust agents that adapt in real time.

In Summary, orchestration tools like Semantic Kernel, LangGraph, and others provide a much-needed bridge between protocol-level communication (enabled by MCP) and high-level agent reasoning and control flow. By layering these orchestration systems atop MCP infrastructure, developers can design AI systems that are not only modular and context-aware but also reactive, scalable, and maintainable—paving the way for real-world AI autonomy.

16.4 Breaking Down Complex Tasks Across Agents

As AI systems evolve to solve more sophisticated problems, it becomes increasingly inefficient—both computationally and architecturally—for a single agent to handle large, multi-step tasks alone. Instead, a more scalable approach involves decomposing complex objectives into smaller, manageable subtasks, each handled by a specialized agent or module. This not only improves clarity and fault isolation but also allows for parallel execution, better reuse of capabilities, and easier debugging. The Model Context Protocol (MCP) plays a central role here by enabling seamless, standardized communication between these agents, regardless of their implementation details.

Consider a scenario where an AI system is tasked with generating a market intelligence report. This overarching goal involves fetching data from APIs, cleaning and structuring it, performing sentiment analysis, drafting summaries, and finally formatting the results into a publishable report. Attempting to handle all of this in a single agent would result in bloated prompt logic, degraded context handling, and poor maintainability. Instead, breaking it into distinct agents—each MCP-compatible—streamlines the process.

Here's how this can be decomposed:

1. **Data Retrieval Agent**: Responsible for fetching real-time market data from multiple APIs (stock prices, economic indicators, news feeds). It uses `mcp.resources` to define external data endpoints and wraps them in tools for LLM accessibility.
2. **Cleaning and Structuring Agent**: Receives raw data, applies transformations and validations (e.g., removing duplicates, converting to structured formats), and exposes these as MCP `tools`.
3. **Sentiment Analysis Agent**: Analyzes the structured content using LLM-based or traditional sentiment models. It is triggered via MCP function calls like `sentiment.analyze`.
4. **Summary Agent**: Composes a coherent report draft using templated prompts and can chain output from previous agents.

5. **Finalizer Agent**: Polishes and formats the document for publication—perhaps adding charts, bullet points, or markdown formatting.

This breakdown lets each agent specialize and scale independently, while MCP acts as the glue ensuring a shared context and predictable interfaces. Let's look at a simplified implementation snippet for invoking such a chain from a coordinator process:

```python
from mcp_client import import MCPClient

client = MCPClient("http://localhost:8000")

async def build_report():
    # Step 1: Fetch market data
    market_data = await client.acall("market.fetch_data",
{"symbols": ["AAPL", "TSLA", "GOOGL"]})

    # Step 2: Clean and structure the data
    structured_data = await client.acall("market.clean_data",
{"raw": market_data})

    # Step 3: Perform sentiment analysis
    sentiment = await client.acall("analysis.sentiment",
{"data": structured_data})

    # Step 4: Generate summary
    summary = await client.acall("report.generate_summary", {
        "data": structured_data,
        "sentiment": sentiment
    })

    # Step 5: Format final report
    final_report = await client.acall("report.format",
{"content": summary})

    return final_report
```

Each MCP method call here corresponds to a distinct tool owned by a specific agent. Because of MCP's standardized JSON-RPC interface and namespaced method semantics, every call is clean, predictable, and modular. Moreover, because each component is isolated, retrying failed stages or rerunning individual tools during debugging becomes trivial.

171

In advanced implementations, these agents can even coordinate among themselves. For example, if the `summary` agent detects gaps in the input, it could invoke the `data` agent directly via MCP to fetch more details. This kind of **agent-to-agent collaboration** is what makes MCP an enabler of truly modular, intelligent systems.

To wrap up, decomposing complex tasks into MCP-powered agents enables not just scalability and reusability, but also unlocks parallelism and clear responsibility boundaries. This mirrors the design principles of distributed systems: small, well-defined components with strong interfaces that collaborate through standardized contracts—exactly what MCP is designed to provide.

16.5 Failure Handling and Recovery in Agent Chaining

In multi-agent systems built on top of the Model Context Protocol (MCP), chaining agents together introduces opportunities for powerful orchestration—but also for cascading failures. If one agent in a chain returns malformed output, times out, or throws an exception, it can disrupt the entire workflow unless failure handling is designed in from the outset. Recovery strategies must therefore be proactive, contextual, and—where possible—automated. MCP's JSON-RPC-based structure makes it easier to diagnose and handle these failures with standardized responses and consistent communication patterns.

At the core of MCP's robustness is its adherence to the JSON-RPC 2.0 specification, which mandates structured error responses. Every method invocation can return either a successful result or an `error` object containing a standardized `code`, `message`, and optional `data`. This design allows orchestrators and agent coordinators to react to issues predictably and take corrective actions based on the type of failure.

Let's explore a practical example involving a three-step agent chain for document analysis: (1) extract text from a file, (2) summarize the text, and (3) generate follow-up questions. Suppose the summarization agent occasionally fails due to prompt overload (too much input) or a service timeout. You might build a recovery layer that retries with trimmed input or skips summarization and logs the issue, allowing the pipeline to continue with degraded functionality.

Here's a simplified MCP interaction with failure handling logic:

172

```python
from mcp_client import import MCPClient, MCPError

client = MCPClient("http://localhost:8000")

async def analyze_document(file_path):
    try:
        extracted_text = await
client.acall("doc.extract_text", {"path": file_path})
    except MCPError as e:
        raise RuntimeError(f"Extraction failed: {e.message}")

    try:
        # Attempt summarization
        summary = await client.acall("doc.summarize",
{"text": extracted_text})
    except MCPError as e:
        if e.code == -32000 and "TooLong" in e.message:
            # Retry with truncated input
            short_text = extracted_text[:1000]
            summary = await client.acall("doc.summarize",
{"text": short_text})
        else:
            # Log and proceed with raw text
            summary = "Summary unavailable due to agent
error."

    try:
        questions = await
client.acall("doc.generate_questions", {"text": summary})
    except MCPError as e:
        questions = ["Could not generate questions due to
error: " + e.message]

    return {
        "summary": summary,
        "questions": questions
    }
```

This structure handles errors at each step without terminating the entire flow. It demonstrates several best practices for agent chaining under MCP:

1. **Explicit try/except blocks for each agent call**: Treat each agent as a fault domain. Isolate failures to keep others unaffected.

2. **Use of standardized `MCPError`**: Catch and inspect the error object's `code` and `message` to apply targeted recovery logic.
3. **Fallbacks and retries**: When appropriate, retry with reduced or modified input rather than halting execution.
4. **Graceful degradation**: If an agent fails but isn't critical to final output (e.g., question generation), proceed and notify the user or log the issue for postmortem analysis.

Additionally, MCP enables logging and traceability through correlation IDs passed in the `params`, allowing failures to be traced across tools and sessions. Combined with observability features (discussed in earlier chapters), this makes it possible to build robust agent workflows that heal themselves or provide actionable diagnostics when something goes wrong.

In Summary, failure handling in agent chaining isn't just about writing exception handlers—it's about designing your system to expect imperfection. MCP's structured communication model gives developers the tools to identify, isolate, and recover from errors without sacrificing workflow continuity. When used thoughtfully, it allows agentic systems to behave with resilience and autonomy, even in real-world, failure-prone environments.

Chapter 17: Governance and Ethics

17.1 Data Privacy and PII Management

As developers build MCP-enabled AI agents capable of ingesting, analyzing, and generating content based on contextual data, handling Personally Identifiable Information (PII) and maintaining user privacy becomes not only a legal mandate but a foundational requirement for trustworthy AI. The Model Context Protocol, with its context-aware and modular design, allows for fine-grained control over data exposure and transmission, making it well-suited for privacy-preserving agentic systems—if implemented thoughtfully.

Data privacy concerns typically arise when agents process sensitive user inputs, logs, documents, or real-time prompts that include names, addresses, financial records, healthcare data, or behavioral profiles. In jurisdictions like the EU under GDPR, or in California under CCPA, mishandling PII can lead to significant penalties and reputational damage. Therefore, developers must adopt a privacy-by-design mindset from the very beginning.

MCP makes this feasible through several architectural affordances. First, context passed through `Resources` or `params` objects can be inspected, redacted, or encrypted before reaching the agent logic. Developers can implement pre-processing filters that identify and strip out sensitive fields, replacing them with masked placeholders or anonymized tokens.

Here's an example of implementing a simple PII redactor as an MCP-compatible resource before context is delivered to an LLM:

```
import re
from mcp_server import import MCPResource

class PIIRedactor(MCPResource):
    async def resolve(self, params):
        text = params.get("text", "")
        # Naïve redaction: names and email patterns
        text = re.sub(r"\b[A-Z][a-z]+\s[A-Z][a-z]+\b",
"[REDACTED_NAME]", text)
        text = re.sub(r"\b[A-Za-z0-9._%+-]+@[A-Za-z0-9.-
]+\.\w{2,}\b", "[REDACTED_EMAIL]", text)
```

```
return {"text": text}
```

In this resource, before any agent sees the raw text, names and emails are removed. In a production-grade system, such a redactor might use a more advanced Named Entity Recognition (NER) model to sanitize inputs, log what was filtered, and optionally encrypt the original text for auditability or later review—without feeding it into the LLM directly.

In addition to input filtering, output from LLMs should also be scanned for privacy breaches, especially in scenarios where an agent is asked to summarize documents, generate emails, or analyze datasets. MCP tools can enforce output constraints via post-processing hooks before returning results to the calling client or user interface.

Furthermore, agent developers can use session tokens, contextual boundaries, and scoped authentication to ensure that agents only access data relevant to their current task and cannot persist or recall PII across sessions unless explicitly allowed. For example, you might disable memory or set short TTLs (time to live) on session contexts involving sensitive records.

In regulated industries like finance or healthcare, logs involving PII must be scrubbed or stored in encrypted form with restricted access controls. MCP's standardized request-response structure makes it easier to programmatically enforce these policies, using message interception at the JSON-RPC transport layer to mask, log, or deny operations involving flagged data.

To summarize, ensuring privacy and managing PII in MCP-based systems involves:

- Pre-processing context with redaction or anonymization tools
- Post-processing LLM output to prevent privacy leakage
- Enforcing scoped access through role-based controls and session isolation
- Minimizing storage and recall of sensitive data across sessions
- Auditing, logging, and encrypting PII-sensitive flows securely

By thoughtfully leveraging MCP's modular architecture, developers can build AI agents that are not only powerful and context-aware but also privacy-compliant and safe to deploy in real-world, user-facing environments. Responsible AI isn't a feature—it's an obligation, and MCP gives us the tools to meet it head-on.

17.2 Transparency and Agent Explainability

In the era of agentic AI systems, transparency is no longer optional—it is a core design principle. As developers empower large language model (LLM)-based agents with decision-making capabilities using the Model Context Protocol (MCP), it becomes essential to ensure that every output can be traced back to its input, logic, and contextual dependencies. Agent explainability refers to the ability to inspect and understand *why* an agent made a particular decision, chose a tool, or followed a specific path in a chain of actions.

MCP naturally supports explainability through its structured JSON-RPC communication, where each call, context injection, and tool/resource invocation is recorded in discrete, queryable transactions. Unlike opaque end-to-end prompts in traditional LLM setups, MCP agents operate through modular interactions—each one invoking tools, requesting external context, or responding with output. This modularity allows for fine-grained tracing.

Let's explore a hands-on example. Suppose we have an MCP-powered agent that helps users troubleshoot deployment issues in cloud environments. When the user submits a problem like *"My ECS service is not scaling,"* the agent might:

1. Parse the query using an LLM
2. Call a registered tool that checks ECS metrics
3. Retrieve logs via a resource connected to AWS CloudWatch
4. Generate a suggestion based on observed thresholds

With MCP, every step is logged as a JSON-RPC method call. Here's a simplified trace of such a conversation:

```
{
  "method": "tool.check_ecs_metrics",
  "params": {
    "service_name": "prod-app",
    "region": "us-east-1"
  },
  "id": "tool_call_001"
}
```

This is followed by:

```
{
  "method": "resource.fetch_logs",
  "params": {
    "log_group": "/aws/ecs/prod-app",
    "filter": "ScalingFailure"
  },
  "id": "resource_call_002"
}
```

And finally, the LLM might synthesize:

```
{
  "result": "Based on recent logs, ECS failed to scale due to
IAM permission errors. Recommend verifying auto-scaling
roles."
}
```

Now, as a developer or even an end-user with access to logs, you can reconstruct the agent's reasoning step-by-step. This makes it possible to answer the critical question: *"Why did the agent give this advice?"*

To enhance explainability further, developers can instrument the agent to output **rationale** metadata alongside results. For instance, every tool response can include a `"reason"` field, and prompts sent to the LLM can be optionally logged (minus sensitive data). Here's how that might look:

```
{
  "tool": "check_ecs_metrics",
  "result": {
    "cpu_utilization": 92,
    "scaling_triggers": ["cpu > 85 for 5 mins"],
    "reason": "Scaling threshold met, but no new tasks
launched"
  }
}
```

This makes it easier for observability dashboards, developer consoles, or even UI-level agents to render clear explanations.

Another practical technique is maintaining a **call chain visualization**, where every invocation is represented in a graph or tree. This helps debug failures or unintended behavior, and it fosters trust in autonomous systems by showing users *how* decisions are made. While MCP doesn't natively enforce this, it provides all the hooks to build such tooling.

To conclude, agent transparency and explainability in MCP systems are best achieved by:

- Logging all JSON-RPC method calls and responses
- Structuring context and output with traceable metadata
- Including rationales in agent responses
- Building visual trace tools for developers and end users
- Minimizing hidden state or opaque prompt injection

In production environments where AI agents act with autonomy—whether helping users, making business decisions, or driving workflows—explainability isn't a luxury. It's an operational and ethical imperative. MCP gives developers the protocol-level scaffolding to embed explainability into the very foundation of their systems.

17.3 Preventing Misuse and Rogue Behavior

As AI agents become more autonomous, interconnected, and powerful—especially when driven by the Model Context Protocol (MCP)—the risk of unintended consequences, misuse, or rogue behavior grows significantly. Preventing this is not just about ethical responsibility; it's about designing systems that are *resilient*, *observable*, and *constrained by intent*. With MCP, you have the opportunity to enforce safeguards at multiple layers of agent operation: through permissioned tool exposure, controlled context injection, structured protocol boundaries, and real-time observability.

A rogue agent is typically defined as one that either acts outside of its intended scope, misuses available tools or resources, or produces harmful or untrustworthy outputs due to a failure in logic, oversight, or input sanitization. These behaviors can arise from poorly designed prompts, unrestricted access to tools, misconfigured server endpoints, or even malicious exploitation of loosely governed APIs. Fortunately, MCP's architecture provides natural checkpoints for containment.

Start with **tool definition and registration**. Every tool exposed through an MCP server must be explicitly registered with a defined method name, schema, and optional authentication requirements. This makes it impossible for an agent to arbitrarily invent new tool invocations. For example, if the server exposes:

```
{
  "method": "tool.send_email",
  "params": {
    "to": "string",
    "subject": "string",
    "body": "string"
  }
}
```

Then unless you've registered this tool on the server, it cannot be invoked— even if the LLM hallucinates such a capability. This enforces a hard perimeter around functionality.

Second, **context injection via resources** must be sanitized and rate-limited. Suppose you expose a resource that lets the agent query a production SQL database. A rogue prompt or malformed input might try to extract private data or cause cascading queries. You can mitigate this by:

- Pre-validating all input parameters server-side
- Restricting data retrieval by scope (e.g., current user only)
- Enforcing row or time-based filters internally
- Logging and alerting on suspicious query patterns

Third, introduce **execution constraints** on the client. MCP clients—typically LLM-driven frontends or orchestrators—should not allow arbitrary free-form prompts to trigger tool execution without intermediate validation. Use techniques like prompt guards, user-in-the-loop confirmations, or action approval workflows to avoid blind execution. A simple approval chain might include:

1. LLM proposes action based on context
2. Middleware checks against allowlist of method names and parameter bounds
3. If safe, action proceeds; otherwise, it's escalated or blocked

Let's see a practical illustration. Assume a developer builds an agent that helps IT staff restart cloud services. It exposes the following tool:

```
{
```

```
  "method": "tool.restart_service",
  "params": {
    "service_id": "string"
  }
}
```

Without safeguards, the LLM might be tricked—via prompt injection or user query manipulation—into restarting mission-critical services. To prevent this:

- Enforce an internal allowlist of service IDs eligible for restart
- Require a second verification step (e.g., confirm intent)
- Log each attempt and rejection reason
- Set up audit trails for all tool usage

You can also leverage **rate limits, token-based authentication**, and **capability tagging** on each MCP session. For example, a session might be tagged `read-only`, and therefore blocked from invoking any method with a `write` capability.

Finally, maintain real-time observability dashboards and alerts for **unexpected patterns**, such as:

- Sudden tool invocation spikes
- Rapid repeat failures
- Unexpected prompt embeddings
- Unknown method calls

MCP's predictable JSON-RPC structure and clean separation of agent interface from backend logic make this possible.

In summary, preventing misuse and rogue behavior in MCP-based AI agents involves proactive design at all layers:

- Only expose tools/resources the agent should have access to.
- Validate inputs and enforce scope limits server-side.
- Add middleware for approval, rate limiting, and capability filtering.
- Log, monitor, and analyze agent actions continuously.
- Assume the LLM may hallucinate or be tricked—and guard against it.

When you treat your AI agent as a programmable, potentially fallible system rather than a static chatbot, you unlock the ability to embed trust, safety, and reliability directly into its operational contract. MCP enables this by design.

17.4 Logging, Auditing, and Legal Requirements

In any production environment where AI agents interact with tools, users, or sensitive data, logging and auditing are not just operational conveniences—they're fundamental pillars of accountability, security, and legal compliance. When using the Model Context Protocol (MCP) to build and deploy context-aware agents, robust logging must be built into the system from the ground up. MCP's structured, JSON-RPC-based communication model provides a natural foundation for capturing detailed logs at every interaction point—tool invocation, context retrieval, server response, or error generation—making it particularly well-suited for auditability.

Every MCP interaction—whether it's a tool call from an agent, a context request from a resource, or even a handshake initialization—should be logged in a structured format. These logs must include timestamps, session identifiers, method names, input parameters (scrubbed for sensitive data), response payloads, error messages, and latency metrics. For example, when a client initiates a call to a method such as `tool.generate_report`, your logging system should capture something like:

```
{
  "timestamp": "2025-06-09T04:12:34Z",
  "session_id": "abc123",
  "method": "tool.generate_report",
  "params": {
    "report_type": "monthly",
    "user_id": "user-789"
  },
  "response_status": "success",
  "latency_ms": 132,
  "invoked_by": "llm-agent-finance"
}
```

From a **compliance perspective**, this log serves multiple functions. It creates an immutable audit trail to trace agent decisions, it helps debug anomalies or regressions in output behavior, and—depending on your industry—may satisfy regulatory frameworks such as GDPR, HIPAA, SOC 2, or ISO 27001. For instance, in financial services, regulators may require retention of all automated decision logs for a fixed duration, often with role-based access control over who can view or export those logs.

It's important to distinguish **operational logging** from **auditable logging**. Operational logs are designed for developers and ops engineers—verbose, transient, and detailed for debugging. Audit logs, on the other hand, must be tamper-evident, securely stored (e.g., in write-once S3 buckets or append-only databases), and governed by access controls. If your MCP system triggers critical actions like data deletion, account changes, or large-scale reporting, audit trails should be mandatory.

MCP's structure makes this feasible. Each interaction is encapsulated within a well-defined method call, making it easy to instrument middleware that logs every incoming request and outgoing response, even before business logic is invoked. Most production-grade MCP implementations place this logic inside the server transport layer (e.g., FastAPI middleware or Flask decorators) so that nothing escapes visibility.

From a **legal standpoint**, you must be aware of:

- **Data minimization**: Logs must not persist sensitive or personally identifiable information (PII) unless explicitly required and justified. For example, don't log full prompt bodies or user names unless masked or hashed.
- **Retention policies**: Depending on jurisdiction, you may be obligated to retain logs for a minimum or maximum period, with requirements for secure deletion afterward.
- **Consent and transparency**: If user data or behavior is being logged for AI-driven decisions, you may need to disclose this in privacy policies or terms of service.
- **Cross-border data transfer**: Logging infrastructure hosted in another country might constitute international data transfer, invoking additional legal obligations.

For practical implementation, you might integrate:

- **Structured JSON logging** with fields for method name, agent ID, session ID, and latency.
- **Token redaction filters** to prevent logging secrets, credentials, or sensitive content.

- **Tamper-proof log stores** using systems like AWS CloudTrail, Azure Monitor Logs, or even blockchain-style append-only ledgers for high-assurance environments.
- **Monitoring dashboards** to visualize tool usage, failure rates, and audit event frequency.

In summary, proper logging and auditing in an MCP-powered AI system is not optional. It is critical for operational insight, security enforcement, compliance with legal frameworks, and building user trust. MCP provides the technical foundation for this: every action is declarative, method-based, and wrapped in a structure ideal for systematic monitoring. But it's up to you—the developer or architect—to ensure this infrastructure is in place, secure, and governed according to modern compliance standards.

17.5 Global Regulations and What's Next for Agent Governance

As AI agents evolve from experimental tools into critical infrastructure powering finance, healthcare, education, law, and customer service, the regulatory landscape surrounding their deployment is rapidly solidifying. The Model Context Protocol (MCP), by formalizing communication, decision-making, and context exchange across agents, positions itself at the center of these governance conversations. Developers using MCP to build intelligent systems must now contend not only with technical challenges but with evolving global legal requirements, cross-border compliance, and the ethics of autonomous behavior.

Globally, the regulatory frameworks for AI are being shaped around four core pillars: transparency, accountability, safety, and privacy. The European Union's AI Act, for example, introduces a tiered risk-based classification system that imposes strict requirements on systems considered "high risk"—including those used in biometric identification, employment, and education. An MCP-powered agent that makes or supports such decisions must now include explainability mechanisms, context-aware audit trails, and safeguards against bias or misuse. This means your agents cannot remain opaque; every tool invocation, prompt transformation, and response generation must be traceable and, when necessary, justifiable.

The United States, while taking a more fragmented approach, is following suit with sector-specific enforcement. The White House Blueprint for an AI Bill of Rights outlines expectations for safety, notice, and algorithmic fairness, which are rapidly influencing federal procurement and corporate standards. California's Consumer Privacy Act (CCPA), now expanded via CPRA, adds stringent data rights over personal information—rights that directly affect how MCP resources handle and retain context.

Asia presents a diverse environment. China's regulations focus on algorithmic recommendation accountability, requiring disclosures of logic and opt-out options. Meanwhile, Singapore and South Korea are moving towards pro-innovation guardrails that emphasize human-in-the-loop controls, a design pattern MCP natively supports through human-agent review workflows and external tool gating.

For developers and AI architects building with MCP, three emerging themes define what's next for agent governance:

1. Contextual Consent and Use Purpose Declaration:
Future regulations may require agents to declare not just *what* they are doing, but *why*—and MCP is uniquely suited for this. Each method call includes metadata. You can extend this to include fields such as `"intended_use"`, `"data_source_justification"`, and `"legal_basis"` for the action. For instance, an MCP `resource.query_patient_data` method might include a required `"consent_token"` or `"HIPAA_context_id"` parameter to verify legitimacy.

2. Autonomous Boundaries and Safeguards:
There is a global push to establish clearer control layers for autonomous systems. MCP enables externalized context and explicit tool access declarations—making it easier to implement *permission layers*, *manual overrides*, or *agent sandboxing*. You can design your server or gateway so that tools performing regulatory-sensitive actions (like financial approvals) require multi-agent agreement or a signed digital assertion from a human reviewer.

3. Multi-Stakeholder Compliance Ledgering:
Auditing requirements are trending toward immutable, shared, and cross-organizational compliance proofs. In the near future, MCP may evolve to support optional compliance headers or append-only compliance logs—recorded to systems like AWS QLDB or blockchain-based registries. This aligns with trends like the UK's Responsible AI assurance framework and the global push for third-party auditability.

In practical terms, MCP-based systems should begin embedding compliance-oriented design principles today. Include modular trust boundaries, redact PII at the resource layer, encrypt tool logs in transit and at rest, and implement agent-level rate limiting. Prepare for runtime policy injection—where an enterprise's regulatory rules are applied to agents dynamically via MCP resources or config streams.

In closing, agent governance is no longer a distant concern for MCP developers—it's an imminent requirement. Those building with the protocol are uniquely equipped to lead in this space due to MCP's explicit, inspectable design. The next frontier lies in combining this technical transparency with legal readiness—building systems that are not just functional and fast, but fair, accountable, and aligned with the rapidly maturing global AI regulatory fabric.

Part VI – Appendices and Reference Material

Chapter 18: Developer Resources and Companion Material

18.1 Glossary of MCP and AI Agent Terms

To build and maintain effective MCP-based systems, developers must be fluent in the foundational terminology that underpins agent communication, orchestration, and context awareness. This glossary defines the most frequently used terms throughout the book and within the Model Context Protocol (MCP) specification, offering a quick-reference resource for developers working on everything from scratch-built MCP servers to production-grade multi-agent architectures.

MCP (Model Context Protocol)
A JSON-RPC-based communication protocol designed to standardize how agents, tools, and external systems exchange contextual data, trigger actions, and respond across distributed AI systems.

Agent
An autonomous or semi-autonomous software entity powered by a large language model (LLM) or symbolic planner that uses MCP to invoke tools, fetch resources, and act on contextual inputs to complete tasks.

Tool
An executable function exposed over MCP, typically defined as a JSON-RPC method. Tools enable agents to perform real-world tasks, such as making HTTP requests, calling APIs, or manipulating data.

Resource
A non-executable contextual data provider accessible via MCP. Resources allow agents to retrieve structured or unstructured information such as documents, user histories, or domain knowledge.

Prompt Context
The structured data injected into an LLM prompt at runtime, often dynamically retrieved through an MCP resource call. Enables situational reasoning and task personalization.

Invocation
The process of an agent calling a tool or querying a resource via MCP. Each invocation includes method name, parameters, context ID, and optionally a trace or audit ID.

Context ID
A unique identifier used to track a specific conversational or task-related context across multiple calls. Helps preserve memory and continuity in long-running agent interactions.

Session
A bounded period of interaction between an MCP client and server, where state, authentication, and capabilities may persist. Often used in combination with context IDs for multi-step workflows.

Handshake
The initial MCP message exchange where a client declares its capabilities (e.g., streaming support, auth tokens) and receives protocol-level configuration from the server.

JSON-RPC
The underlying protocol that MCP extends and structures. A lightweight, stateless, transport-agnostic protocol using JSON to encode remote procedure calls.

Capability Declaration
A metadata block sent during the handshake or registration phase describing what features an agent, client, or tool supports (e.g., async callbacks, traceability, response streaming).

Trace ID / Audit ID
Optional metadata used to correlate MCP actions for observability or debugging. Typically injected into request headers or metadata fields for downstream logging.

Tool Server
An application or container that hosts MCP-compatible tools and resources. It accepts JSON-RPC requests and responds according to the MCP specification, often via HTTP or WebSocket.

MCP Client
Any application or agent that initiates requests to an MCP server. Clients

may embed LLMs, be part of LangChain, or operate as orchestrators in broader AI pipelines.

External Context
Any data not already known to the LLM that is retrieved at runtime to augment prompts. Can include company policies, product databases, or user preferences retrieved via resources.

Prompt Template
A reusable text or code snippet containing placeholders for dynamic context. Often parameterized to receive MCP resource output for constructing final agent prompts.

Role-Based Agent
An AI agent configured with a specific function (e.g., "Summarizer", "Planner", "Retriever"), often working in coordination with other agents in a multi-agent graph.

Orchestration
The coordination of agent tasks, tool invocations, and context flows—especially across multiple systems. Can involve LangGraph, CrewAI, or custom MCP implementations.

Human-in-the-Loop (HITL)
A control pattern in which a human oversees or approves certain agent actions before they execute, often implemented via resource injection or review tools.

Semantic Kernel, LangChain, CrewAI
Frameworks that integrate with MCP to support task routing, memory, planning, and coordination across agents and external tools.

This glossary continues to expand as the ecosystem matures. Each term here is used consistently throughout the book to avoid ambiguity and reinforce best practices in MCP-based system design. As you proceed through implementation and deployment, refer back to this glossary to ensure clarity and alignment with protocol semantics.

18.2 Full MCP JSON-RPC Protocol Reference

The Model Context Protocol (MCP) builds on the JSON-RPC 2.0 specification by introducing context-awareness, agent metadata, and standardized tooling semantics for AI systems. This section provides a complete technical reference for all core MCP methods, their required parameters, optional fields, expected responses, and usage behavior—based on the official MCP schema and agent interoperability guidelines.

Each method conforms to the JSON-RPC 2.0 request structure, consisting of:

```
{
  "jsonrpc": "2.0",
  "method": "method_name",
  "params": { /* method-specific parameters */ },
  "id": "optional-request-id"
}
```

Below is the structured overview of MCP's main method categories and message structures:

---

context.initialize

Description: Establishes a new MCP session and optionally registers the client's capabilities.

Parameters:

- `session_id` (string, optional): Unique identifier for the session. If omitted, server may assign one.
- `capabilities` (object, optional): Feature declarations (e.g., `"streaming": true`).

Example:

```
{
  "jsonrpc": "2.0",
  "method": "context.initialize",
```

```
    "params": {
      "capabilities": {
        "streaming": true,
        "trace_id_support": true
      }
    },
    "id": 1
}
```

Response:

```
{
  "jsonrpc": "2.0",
  "result": {
    "session_id": "abc123-session",
    "server_capabilities": { "streaming": true }
  },
  "id": 1
}
```

`tool.invoke`

Description: Executes a server-exposed function with input parameters and optional context metadata.

Parameters:

- `name` (string): Tool/function name, e.g., `"search.docs"`.
- `input` (object): Tool-specific input arguments.
- `context_id` (string, optional): Current interaction context.
- `trace_id` (string, optional): For observability/logging.

Example:

```
{
  "jsonrpc": "2.0",
  "method": "tool.invoke",
  "params": {
    "name": "math.calculate",
```

192

```
      "input": { "expression": "2 + 3 * 5" },
      "context_id": "session-xyz"
   },
   "id": 42
}
```

Response:

```
{
   "jsonrpc": "2.0",
   "result": {
      "output": "17"
   },
   "id": 42
}
```

resource.fetch

Description: Retrieves data from an external or internal data source registered with the MCP server.

Parameters:

- `name` (string): Resource identifier, e.g., `"docs.hr_policy"`.
- `filters` (object, optional): Search or filtering criteria.
- `context_id` (string, optional): Interaction context for personalization.
- `trace_id` (string, optional): For audit tracking.

Example:

```
{
   "jsonrpc": "2.0",
   "method": "resource.fetch",
   "params": {
      "name": "docs.company_wiki",
      "filters": { "section": "benefits" }
   },
   "id": 2
```

```
]
```

Response:

```
{
  "jsonrpc": "2.0",
  "result": {
    "data": [
      { "title": "Healthcare Benefits", "text": "All employees
receive..." }
    ]
  },
  "id": 2
}
```

`context.terminate`

Description: Closes the session or cleans up context state.

Parameters:

- `session_id` (string): Session to terminate.
- `reason` (string, optional): Reason for termination.

Example:

```
{
  "jsonrpc": "2.0",
  "method": "context.terminate",
  "params": {
    "session_id": "abc123-session",
    "reason": "task complete"
  },
  "id": 3
}
```

Response:

```
{
  "jsonrpc": "2.0",
  "result": { "status": "terminated" },
  "id": 3
}
```

Error Handling

All MCP method calls conform to JSON-RPC 2.0's error specification:

Error Format:

```
{
  "jsonrpc": "2.0",
  "error": {
    "code": -32000,
    "message": "Tool not found: math.calculate",
    "data": { "hint": "Check tool registration on server" }
  },
  "id": 42
}
```

Common error codes include:

- `-32601`: Method not found
- `-32602`: Invalid params
- `-32000`: MCP execution error
- `-32001`: Resource unavailable
- `-32002`: Unauthorized or unauthenticated request

Notes on Streaming

If the client and server both declare `"streaming"`: `true` during `context.initialize`, the server may respond to `tool.invoke` using chunked messages over WebSocket or HTTP/2 with the same ID but partial data. The final chunk usually contains a `"done"`: `true` flag or closes the connection.

195

Summary

This protocol reference provides the full suite of MCP methods used in both experimental and production systems. When constructing or debugging MCP-based clients and servers, refer to these canonical message formats and adjust your integration logic to conform strictly to expected method structure, context tracking, and JSON-RPC compliance. Following these specifications ensures your AI agents, LLM workflows, and orchestration tools communicate consistently and reliably across distributed environments.

18.3 Standalone Code Snippets and Mini Projects

This section provides a curated set of minimal, self-contained code snippets and mini projects that demonstrate how to work with the Model Context Protocol (MCP) across various real-world scenarios. Each example is crafted to highlight a single concept clearly—whether you're testing a specific method call, exploring local debugging flows, or experimenting with context-aware prompt injection. These are especially useful for developers who want to quickly prototype ideas or understand a particular part of the MCP stack without committing to a full deployment.

Let's begin with a basic MCP tool server that registers a simple calculator function. This example demonstrates how to expose a tool via the `tool.invoke` method using Python with FastAPI and JSON-RPC over HTTP.

```python
# mcp_server.py

from fastapi import FastAPI, Request
from pydantic import BaseModel
from typing import Any, Dict
import uvicorn
import json

app = FastAPI()

# Define expected structure for MCP JSON-RPC requests
class JSONRPCRequest(BaseModel):
    jsonrpc: str
    method: str
```

```python
    params: Dict[str, Any]
    id: Any

@app.post("/")
async def handle_rpc(request: Request):
    body = await request.json()
    req = JSONRPCRequest(**body)

    if req.method == "tool.invoke" and req.params.get("name") == "math.add":
        input_data = req.params.get("input", {})
        x = input_data.get("x", 0)
        y = input_data.get("y", 0)
        result = x + y
        return {
            "jsonrpc": "2.0",
            "result": {"output": result},
            "id": req.id
        }

    return {
        "jsonrpc": "2.0",
        "error": {
            "code": -32601,
            "message": f"Method not found: {req.method}"
        },
        "id": req.id
    }

if __name__ == "__main__":
    uvicorn.run("mcp_server:app", host="0.0.0.0", port=8000)
```

You can run this with:

```
python mcp_server.py
```

And then send a JSON-RPC request using `curl` or Postman:

```
curl -X POST http://localhost:8000/ \
  -H "Content-Type: application/json" \
  -d '{
        "jsonrpc": "2.0",
        "method": "tool.invoke",
        "params": {
```

```
        "name": "math.add",
        "input": {"x": 7, "y": 3}
      },
      "id": 1
    }'
```

Expected response:

```
{
  "jsonrpc": "2.0",
  "result": {
    "output": 10
  },
  "id": 1
}
```

This mini project gives you a complete round-trip: tool registration, method routing, and parameter handling—all within one file. You can expand it by supporting other tool names, implementing `resource.fetch`, or layering in authentication logic as needed.

Next, consider a lightweight MCP client call example using Python to test the server:

```
# mcp_client.py

import requests

payload = {
    "jsonrpc": "2.0",
    "method": "tool.invoke",
    "params": {
        "name": "math.add",
        "input": {"x": 5, "y": 9}
    },
    "id": 99
}

response = requests.post("http://localhost:8000/",
json=payload)
print(response.json())
```

Running this script shows immediate feedback, letting you test connectivity, error handling, and output formatting without needing a full orchestration pipeline.

Each snippet in this appendix is designed for fast experimentation. Whether you're writing an internal tool, building LLM pipelines, or teaching others how JSON-RPC works in an MCP context, these standalone code blocks serve as excellent springboards.

In future editions, we may include language-specific clients, WebSocket-based streaming samples, and integrations with lightweight frontends for prompt execution. For now, feel free to extend these snippets to fit your environment, iterate quickly, and build production-ready features from these small, reliable foundations.

18.4 Troubleshooting Cheatsheets and Checklists

Even the most robust MCP-enabled system can run into issues—failed RPC calls, missing context, malformed prompts, or authentication errors. This section provides concise troubleshooting guidance and diagnostic checklists to help developers debug, stabilize, and optimize MCP-powered agents in both local development and production environments.

Common Issues and Fixes

1. JSON-RPC Parsing Failures

- **Symptom**: You see an error like `Parse error` or `Invalid JSON was received by the server`.
- **Checklist**:
    - o Validate the JSON syntax (e.g., no trailing commas).
    - o Ensure `jsonrpc` is set to `"2.0"` exactly.
    - o Confirm required fields like `method`, `params`, and `id` are present.

2. "Method Not Found" Errors

- **Symptom**: Response includes `-32601: Method not found`
- **Checklist**:

- Ensure the method name (e.g., `tool.invoke`, `resource.fetch`) is correctly spelled.
- Verify the server exposes a handler for that method.
- Double-check that the handler is reachable on the correct endpoint.

3. Tool or Resource Name Not Recognized

- **Symptom**: Server responds but says `Unknown tool name: xyz.tool`
- **Checklist**:
  - Confirm that the `name` inside `params` matches an exposed tool/resource.
  - Check registration code in the server—was the tool actually defined?
  - Restart the server after adding a new tool or resource.

4. Input Parameters Are Ignored or Cause Crashes

- **Symptom**: Server throws an internal error or returns incorrect outputs.
- **Checklist**:
  - Inspect the `input` payload inside `params`; make sure it contains expected keys.
  - Use default fallbacks in your tool implementation to avoid `NoneType` issues.
  - Use `pydantic` models to validate structure if your server supports it.

5. Authentication Token Errors

- **Symptom**: Request fails with 401 Unauthorized or similar.
- **Checklist**:
  - Verify that the token is passed correctly in headers (e.g., `Authorization: Bearer <token>`).
  - Confirm server-side logic checks the token and is not rejecting valid sessions.
  - Ensure the token hasn't expired or been revoked.

6. Timeout or No Response

- **Symptom**: The client waits indefinitely or times out after many seconds.
- **Checklist**:
    o Check server logs to confirm whether the request was received.
    o Test the same endpoint with `curl` to see if the delay persists.
    o Use a profiler or logger to detect long-running operations in the handler.

7. Unexpected Output Format

- **Symptom**: LLM or downstream systems don't understand the response.
- **Checklist**:
    o Make sure `result` is wrapped inside the expected format: `{"output": <value>}`.
    o Validate JSON output against the schema expected by the client.
    o Avoid sending non-serializable Python objects like sets or custom classes.

Developer's Daily Debug Checklist

Before shipping or pushing updates to an MCP agent workflow, review this quick checklist:

Is your server running and listening on the correct port?
Are your tools and resources registered with correct `name` strings?
Are all requests using the `"jsonrpc": "2.0"` field?
Do all response payloads return either a `result` or an `error`, but not both?
Are timeouts, retries, and fallbacks configured for remote calls?
Are logs detailed and timestamped, with clear traces for each request ID?
Have you tested a degraded network condition or resource outage?

Production Hardening Tips

Once your system is live, these best practices help reduce risk and aid future debugging:

- Enable request/response logging, including IDs and timestamps.
- Capture metrics for tool latency and failure rates (e.g., via Prometheus or OpenTelemetry).
- Use structured logging (JSON format) for easy searching and correlation.
- Isolate sensitive context payloads in logs and redact PII.
- Run unit tests on each tool/resource before deployment.
- Establish health check endpoints and readiness probes.

By using this cheatsheet and checklist, developers can dramatically reduce the time spent diagnosing MCP integration bugs. Whether you're building a LangChain bridge, an AutoGPT workflow, or a custom AI assistant, consistent request formats, strong logging practices, and deliberate validation of inputs and outputs are your strongest allies in keeping your agents stable and reliable.

18.5 Update Notes, Future Editions, and Reader Feedback

This section serves as your hub for understanding how the content in this book evolves over time, how to stay current with MCP developments, and how you as a reader can shape future editions through feedback and contributions. Since the Model Context Protocol (MCP) and surrounding agentic infrastructure are rapidly evolving, it's critical that our learning resources remain just as dynamic and responsive.

Update Notes

Each print or digital version of this book may contain revisions, updates, or clarifications based on:

- Evolving MCP protocol specifications
- Tooling changes (e.g., updates to the MCP SDK or JSON-RPC handler libraries)

- New best practices from the field
- Bug fixes or outdated content corrections
- Community feedback highlighting unclear sections or outdated examples

Version numbers for each edition will be reflected in the book's front matter and the appendix changelog. A snapshot of major changes in this edition includes:

- Revised MCP interaction diagrams for clarity
- Updated code snippets for `tool.invoke`, `resource.fetch`, and client connection logic
- Refined deployment sections for AWS, Azure, and GCP based on new SDK versions
- Expanded walkthroughs for LangChain and AutoGPT integrations

Future Editions: What's Coming Next?

We are already planning the roadmap for future editions of *MCP AI: A Developer's Guide to Building NextGen AI Agents*. These may include:

- A new section dedicated to **OpenAI Agents SDK + MCP integration**
- Deep dive into **PEP-style extension proposals** for future MCP evolution
- Full-featured **MCP testing and mocking framework**
- Expanded real-world deployment walkthroughs using **Docker Compose**, **Helm**, and **Terraform**
- Companion CLI tool to scaffold and validate MCP-compatible agent servers

We aim to keep the content evergreen by focusing on modular updates—individual chapters may be reworked and released as standalone supplements before rolling into a full new edition.

Reader Feedback and Contribution

Your feedback is not only welcome—it's essential. Whether you're a developer encountering an issue, a team implementing MCP at scale, or a reader finding a section confusing or incomplete, we want to hear from you. Here's how you can contribute to making this book better:

- **Corrections**: Found a typo or a code issue? Let us know so we can fix it in the next update.
- **Suggestions**: Have an idea for a new section, architecture pattern, or real-world use case? We'll consider including it in future printings.
- **Testimonials and Case Studies**: If you've implemented MCP in production, we're actively seeking contributors for case study sections in the next edition.
- **Technical Reviews**: If you are a domain expert, reach out about participating in peer review or pre-release feedback for the next edition.

To provide feedback, use the email or contact form noted in the preface of this book. We regularly review and respond to serious submissions, and some contributors may be credited in future editions.

Closing Thoughts

This book is not static—it's part of a living ecosystem. The MCP standard itself is growing through community discussions, implementation feedback, and real-world pressures. As this protocol matures, we are committed to maintaining a guide that reflects its best practices, explains its complexity with clarity, and helps every developer—from hobbyist to enterprise engineer—build smarter, more context-aware AI agents.

Your voice, use cases, and field experience help guide where this journey goes next. Let's continue building it together.

www.ingramcontent.com/pod-product-compliance
Lightning Source LLC
LaVergne TN
LVHW081525050326
832903LV00025B/1630